Classic Kitchens *for* Modern Living

Sarah Blank Design Studio

Classic Kitchens *for* Modern Living

images
Publishing

Contents

7 **Prologue**   11 **Foreword**   13 **Introduction**

20 A Thank You Letter to Bunny Williams

24 Picturesque Family Heirlooms | Litchfield Hills, Connecticut

40 Majestic Hudson River Valley | Irvington, New York

54 Bridging the Past and Future | Bronxville, New York

70 A Special Place in Bedford | Bedford, New York

86 Mediterranean in Connecticut | Darien, Connecticut

98 A Classic Beauty | Scarsdale, New York

114 Family Memories and Traditions | Sharon, Connecticut

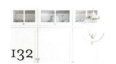 132 Transformed and Treasured | Darien, Connecticut

 144 French Revival with Flair | Darien, Connecticut

 154 Palm Beach Lifestyle | Palm Beach, Florida

 166 Mediterranean Moroccan | New Rochelle, New York

 178 Gracious Georgian Home | Stamford, Connecticut

 190 Classically Detailed in Darien | Darien, Connecticut

 206 American Farmhouse Dream | New Canaan, Connecticut

220 **Acknowledgments**   221 **Project Credits**

Prologue

In every beautiful home I have known—and I count many of the Hudson River Valley's masterpieces, both historic and contemporary, among them—I have been awed by sitting rooms, stair halls, chambers, dining rooms, and more. But there is one room that perhaps presents a unique challenge to any designer: the kitchen. It is here that a certain amount of magic must be conjured to achieve that elusive balance of style and substance.

Sarah's approach to that singularly demanding room happily results in successes that are as beautiful as they are practical. The combination of her design smarts, her thorough consideration of the client's needs, and her deep appreciation for both material and craftsmanship means that each and every example in this book is a small masterclass unto itself on the art of kitchen design.

What's more, Sarah's supreme sensitivity to architectural context is an essential ingredient to interiors that so perfectly complement their surroundings. These are kitchens built to last. Thoughtful designs will allow them to be enjoyed for generations, and their flawless integration into both historic and new homes ensures a welcome continuity of architectural and design languages. In particular, Sarah's projects in my beloved Hudson River Valley admirably complement, and even enhance, both the region's architectural and natural beauty.

Finally, I can't overstate the sheer pleasure of turning each page in this book and encountering so many incredible projects, all beautifully photographed and simply brimming with inventiveness, refined craftsmanship, and of course Sarah's remarkable eye for design.

To journey through this remarkable collection of truly refined kitchens, dining nooks, wine cellars, and more is to observe a great talent at work, deftly blending tradition and elegance with utility and ease. Let there be no doubt that the following pages reveal a master at work!

Peter Lyden, president of the Institute of Classical Architecture & Art

"It has been a delight to collaborate with Sarah Blank on many kitchen designs over the years. Her understanding of the practical and working aspects of the kitchen cannot be matched and her sense of design and architecture create kitchens that perfectly fit the individual, establishing her as one of the very best kitchen designers working today."

—*Bunny Williams*

Foreword

The kitchen is without a doubt one of the most complex design challenges in a house. Unlike kitchens of the past, today we ask a kitchen to satisfy all of the practicalities of food preparation for a family, to be a gathering place, and to be beautiful. To that measure, Sarah Blank has always placed the beauty and functionality of the final design at the very top of her priorities. This requires a creative mind that can balance the special needs of a household, a thorough knowledge of the equipment, materials, and fixtures, and, above all, a special eye for providing a beautiful cohesion to it all.

Sarah's in-depth expertise is an invaluable resource for individual homeowners as well as seasoned professionals. As an architect, I can attest that it is difficult for us to be able to be on top of all of the latest products and trends on the market. Sarah and her talented team are sought-after industry professionals, continuing to provide homeowners, architects, and designers with a high level of expertise, knowledge, and experience in kitchen design. The proof is in the pudding, as they say, and so it is, that in the pages of this book, you will see how Sarah Blank Design Studio is able to bring practicality, durability, and beauty together in the kitchen.

Anne Fairfax, AIA, RIBA

Fairfax & Sammons

Introduction

I grew up in a modest Georgian home nestled alongside the seventh fairway of the Country Club of Waterbury. I recall the day my father decided to fulfill my mother's dream of a grand kitchen. We lived with a small L-shaped kitchen located in the back of the house, until a large rear addition would transform the space. The excitement of seeing my parents collaborate on how to be most comfortable working in the kitchen, while simultaneously spending quality family time stays with me. It was then that I realized the kitchen could, and should, be the center of the home. Our kitchen enhanced the overall aesthetic of the home, rather than detracted from it. Today our house still stands, replete with its historic charm, and an efficiently working kitchen at the center of it all.

My ensuing journey throughout forty years of designing kitchens, baths, and butler's pantries has fueled my passion for the language of classicism and integrating the classical principles into my projects. Classicism's historic longevity speaks to its value in the twenty-first century. To study fine architectural millwork and understand the level of restraint and simplicity required to achieve proper proportion is a learned skill requiring intention and dedication. Exquisite details, proportions, and compositions resonate with me because they are the foundation of the spaces that excite me most. I strongly believe in approaching design through classicism, capitalizing on its inherent adaptability within all spaces utilized in the modern lifestyle. This book intends to share the uniqueness of my approach and the importance of the classic home. Classic spaces work for modern living because their principles stand the test of time.

I was introduced to fine furniture and design as a young child. My father, a physician, had hobbies that included furniture making, American history, and growing a formal rose garden that contained historical plants originally brought to this country by Thomas Jefferson. My childhood vacations never included a day at the beach. We were forever visiting Monticello, Winterthur Museum and Garden, and Mount Vernon. Those impressions were my early education. Thomas Jefferson was pivotal in shaping much of the architecture in America today and undoubtedly the American landscape as we know it.

My high school history teacher, whom I admired greatly, saw my interest in art and architecture and introduced me to his uncle Richard Knapple, the head of the interior design department at Bloomingdales at the time. Richard hired me for the summer before my freshman year at college and directed me to the Fashion Institute of Technology for interior design. Entrenched in the four-year program, American architecture always proved to be my most passionate subject. Kitchen design was not taught at the time, so it remained an unknown entity. My first career position was with a European kitchen firm based in the A&D Building in New York, and so it all began.

In general, studying the history of kitchen design is a challenge. Early records are nonexistent. Most initial documentation lists the kitchen as a room built in the basement, or outbuildings for the sole purpose of food preparation, not living or entertaining. Integrating a kitchen into the architecture and scheme of a quality home was not taught in design schools, primarily because doing so was not standard practice. Kitchens of the mid-twentieth century and earlier are not representative of kitchens today.

The lack of history for a kitchen to complement classic houses creates a predicament for modern homes of this style. The "classic kitchen" is a relatively new frontier in attempting to create a new kitchen that will exist cohesively with a centuries-old fashion. Working within the existing architecture, coupled with the complexity of twenty-first-century amenities, makes this task a challenge. But in that challenge I have built my career and one fact is clear: The kitchen, once relegated to an outside building banished from the main house and where the family feared to tread, has moved inside and evolved into the hub of the home and a welcome gathering space for family and friends. (And moving bathrooms once exiled to the outhouse to the lavish interior spaces we see today is another book!)

Connecting one of contemporary America's most important rooms to the historical significance of classical architecture and design creates harmony between front-of-house and back-of-house rooms. This connection and transition complete the design of a home and give it a cohesive visual language. Classicism offers an opportunity to move with delight from room to room, inside to outside. That invitation includes the kitchen. The importance of this complex room demands and deserves solid knowledge of the past so that it can connect to the rest of the house, and to its future purpose. Recognizing and incorporating history into its development creates fine architectural rooms.

My style is distinguishable from other kitchen designers because I believe in the importance of carrying a home's aesthetic into these back-of-house spaces, and I firmly adhere to the principles of classicism. By studying classical architecture dating back to Vitruvius, Palladio, Jefferson, William Lawrence Bottomley, and McKim, Mead & White, as well as having the good fortune to work with prominent designers and architects in practice today (including Phillip James Dodd, Fairfax & Sammons, Ferguson & Shamamian Architects, G. P. Schafer Architect, and Bunny Williams Interior Design), I have incorporated a set of rules and principles in my work that are imperative to beautiful and functional design, mastering some of the finest kitchens ever developed for a new generation of happy homeowners. I am most gratified by seeing how the beauty and function of a completed kitchen is enjoyed by a family as they make happy memories in a space that will welcome and serve them for many years to come.

Hollyhock, designed with Bunny Williams.

A Thank You Letter to Bunny Williams

I was first introduced to Bunny Williams in September 1999 when a previous client in Bedford, New York, referred me to a new interior design project that Bunny would be doing. I never could have anticipated how that phone call would change the trajectory of my career, and better yet, mark the start of a meaningful twenty-year friendship.

That fateful call came from Bunny Williams's office to ask me if I would work with Bunny on the kitchen design for a house in Cleveland, Ohio. Indeed, I agreed, and embarked on an adventure of learning, collaboration, and admiration that is cherished and rare in anyone's career. Everyone should be so lucky to have such a stalwart champion of others, who is so generous with her knowledge, and such a joy to know.

I have Bunny to thank repeatedly and sincerely for sharing her expertise, which allowed me to elevate my career and my appreciation for the wonderful industry in which we work. Bunny is a leader in every sense of the word, and I cannot imagine America's interior design industry without her stewardship and spirit. For the past two decades, she has included me on numerous projects that helped me develop my professional skills and apply my creative side to projects I am proud to say I had a part in.

I vividly recall many meetings with different clients and coming away from each having learned from Bunny some new perspective or pearl of wisdom. I gave all to my role in every project, offering the team my expertise, but I always felt that I received the better part of the deal. I was learning from Bunny.

I have so many great memories over the years of working with Bunny and her talented, visionary team. I continue to be in touch with Bunny and the many designers that worked for her. She was and is a beacon and a mentor to so many.

This chapter is dedicated to Bunny Williams, who I wholeheartedly thank for all that she has taught me and the valuable lessons she has given me, regardless of their difficulty. She has been there for me ever since we met all those years ago. An education from Bunny, it seems, must be the "Harvard" of the design world!

Hickory Hill, designed with Bunny Williams.

Hickory Hill, designed with Bunny Williams.

Bunny is merely an email or phone call away to lend her insights, if ever I need advice. The design industry, as well as any industry, could use more leaders like her.

Not only is Bunny easy to work with, she is extremely practical and knowledgeable about how to put a project together. She has the client's best interests in mind as she listens carefully to their needs and guides them skillfully through the process, achieving beautiful results that have made her a beloved and admired industry legend.

Her devotion to the Institute of Classical Architecture & Art has inspired me, as I'm also passionate about supporting the organization, with its mission so dear to my heart. Bunny inherently understands every nuance of the classical language and the importance of good design right from the start. For every project, she assembles a team of only the best professionals, and I feel honored and greatly appreciative that I have been a part of her ensemble. As an ardent classicist myself, working on projects that demand that high level of understanding and commitment to the holistic vision is the kind of challenge that motivates my work day-to-day. Some of the most renowned work I have done is on projects with Bunny, and I am delighted to share my favorites in this book.

An integral part of Bunny's character, and what makes her inspirational to all, is Bunny's devotion to causes that improve the larger community. She is a tireless and essential advocate and contributor to the Kips Bay Boys & Girls Club, one of the finest organizations that cares for underprivileged children, and she has lent the full force of her talent and resources to bring people and resources to support that great cause.

Bunny's career is one to admire and inspire, and I love being a part of it. I am better for knowing her.

Bunny, thank you so much.

Picturesque Family Heirlooms

CONTEMPORARY FARMHOUSE | LITCHFIELD HILLS, CONNECTICUT

Litchfield Hills of Connecticut exemplifies the breathtaking scenery celebrated in New England landscapes. With charming small towns and picturesque natural surroundings, they represent a unique destination with plenty to offer. The colonial architecture, stunning farmland, rolling hills, deep woods, and quiet country roads are a few of the region's many redeeming qualities. I highly recommend anyone visit the Litchfield Hills as a highlight of a quintessentially American area.

Nestled in these picturesque Litchfield Hills was an existing colonial-style house surrounded by extensive acreage of fields and woods. A couple fond of the area purchased the house, recognizing its unique offering as a country home, and with hopes it would be filled and enjoyed by their growing family. They called Bunny Williams to work on the design and decoration of their new home, and she invited me to collaborate on the project with her and architect Mark Ferguson of Ferguson & Shamamian Architects. Bunny understands the importance of function, and she has a profound talent for making it beautiful. Bunny and Mark's team transformed this home into the most gorgeous country compound one could imagine, and I felt honored to design the kitchen and pantry. I am always privileged to work with a team of such skilled professionals who understand and appreciate the details that each expert contributes to the collaborative process, which ultimately results in a stronger final project.

My starting point for the way a space should function is to spend time with the homeowner. Do they have young children? Are they someone who entertains? Do they collect objects and fine art? Is the homeowner a passionate chef or do they have a cook?

The homeowner is a wonderful cook, so I wanted to make sure that every inch of space in the kitchen worked optimally for her. Functionality at every level was imperative, as this kitchen would be an essential feature and frequently used space in the home.

I like to get to know all of my clients so I can design their space in a way that supports how they live. To understand them better, I take inventory of every item they own to see how everything can fit seamlessly into the result they envision. First impressions of a room are made on aesthetics. But real appreciation of a room and its success are in the way it functions and the details one doesn't see, such as storage.

Once I have solid knowledge of the client's needs, the overarching design must be thought out and the layout configured into relevant functional stations, such as cooking, washing, food preparation, and storage. Each station needs to be complete and serve its purpose. Any weak links could impact the overall design integrity. My layout process for a space begins at the ceiling, then subsequentially ventures downward, creating a master design plan through a bird's-eye view perspective. The major appliances and sinks are often the functioning anchor piece of a station, and hoods and pendant lights need to be considered at the beginning so that wiring is coordinated. Working from the top down is necessary for the form and function to have harmony.

In this home, the addition of a breakfast room and pushing the west wall back translated into more space for the kitchen. Mark and his team created two additional pantries and a paneled jamb that allowed for essential extra storage. An outsider might judge the different rooms and closets as appearing disjointed, though this is quite the contrary. Designing spaces that fit the functionality specific to the residents' lifestyles is always a priority. If you know your client and understand how they work, you recognize each room plays a unique role for them. Along with the multiple pantries in this home, I was able to categorize each area for how it would be best utilized, and each cabinet and drawer space was allocated for the client's inventory. Deep drawers front to back provide ample pot and pan storage, and the large island provides plenty of countertop for food preparation.

PICTURESQUE FAMILY HEIRLOOMS 27

All the design decisions we arrive at are the result of a meticulous process. We refer to this stage as design development. There is a necessary methodology that we go through to reach a final, successful outcome, and there are no short cuts. In sharing practical advice, if you take shortcuts or fail to take the time to design every inch of the space, then you will undoubtedly make a mistake or miss a crucial detail that compromises the success of a project. It may look beautiful from the outside, but not function well on the inside.

In addition to the three primary stations, other designated areas were incorporated into the overall design, including a baking pantry, dish storage area, and dog station. I knew when we unpacked this kitchen that we had properly sized areas designated for fine dishes, everyday dishes, and for every pot, pan, and tray. There is a coffee station with a space for the mugs, which I located in the top drawer under the counter.

It's fun to think creatively how to find and utilize space and I love it when I have a paneled jamb with tall storage. One thinks they are entering a room with panels to the left and right, which adds character and beautifully disguises wonderful tall storage. In this kitchen the paneled jamb cabinets were not wide enough to make glass display cabinets, but they turned out to be a perfect location for a vacuum, step ladder, and brooms. On the other side there are roll outs that conveniently hold small appliances, such as a juicer or blender.

Pro Tips

Calculate storage needs to the inch

The size of every shelf, drawer, and cupboard needs to be calculated so that it will comfortably accommodate what will be stored inside it, and to ensure maximum efficiency and functionality.

A base cabinet is usually 24 inches deep. A drawer inside would be 21 inches deep based on the drawer track sizes. Thus, the cabinet drawer will only accommodate two larger size pots on the diagonal and perhaps one or two small ones. We prefer to specify a base cabinet 27 inches deep so that it has a longer track and deeper drawer, (front to back) providing space to store substantial-size pots.

Drawer height and custom divider inserts are necessary for a kitchen to function well. Drawers should be partitioned properly to store utensils of different size. For example, ladles and spatulas require more height than cutlery or wooden spoons. Think through what will be stored where, and locate these items during the design process.

A shelf for platters should be a minimum of 18 inches deep, and as wide as it can be without compromising the support. I like to include partitions for storing platters (and other items) vertically. I have never found stacking platters on top of each other to work well.

Large cutting boards should be stored in a convenient location close to the sink. Sometimes I will partition off a 6- to 8-inch section under the sink cabinet for storing cutting boards vertically. Larger ones may also be stored above the oven cabinet where you have great depth and height.

Shelves in most standard wall cabinets are 12 inches apart and 12 inches deep. To accommodate dishes and wider glasses on the shelves we specify wall cabinets at a minimum of 15 inches deep if the space is available. This allows for a 13- to 13.5-inch-deep shelf, which is a much more versatile storage size.

Wine glasses can be very tall. Most red wine glasses are 9 to 10 inches in height, and the widest part of the glass can range from 2.5 to 3.75 inches. Therefore, three glasses deep can fit on a standard 12-inch-deep shelf. A shelf depth of 13.5 inches will allow greater space for storing a full set of wine glasses.

Pantry shelves with 12-inch height is limiting. We allow 15 inches on some pantry shelves for storing taller items such as vases, pitchers, or lobster pots. The perfect pantry allows for a gradation of shelf depth and height clearance.

Beauty has its own special place in making a pleasing environment loved by the homeowner. The design team created that beauty through the juxtaposition of rustic, textured materials and fine, elegant millwork. One is first struck by the heft and rough cut of the hand-hewn beams that maintain the contemporary farmhouse character, and the cathedral ceiling that provides the dramatic height. This formation allows for unobstructed views from the back of the house facing Litchfield Hills. Nature's palette, such as the surrounding birch trees, provided the basis for the warm white cabinet finish. The refined and elegant custom millwork respects architectural traditions, and is a contrast to the rawness of the natural wood beams and stone walls. We selected a hood in keeping with the farmhouse character. Both the metal finish on the hood and the hardware have a heaviness and matte finish, yet provide some contrast and draw the eye.

Bunny is a master and never fails to amaze me. The brightness and warmth of color and furniture keep the area deceptively simple. Each detail is well thought out and layered with texture, color, or pattern that is comfortable and inviting, providing a bright and cheery breakfast area. Though cabinetry and countertops may not be thought of by

some as "furniture," they are typically the presiding elements in the kitchen, and must work with the overall interior design for a space to feel cohesive. I enjoy the challenge of color and details, such as trim or hardware. In the same way pillows or lamps imbue personality in a design, it is all part of creating a seamless décor.

Selecting the various surfaces and appliances is always where I look at how each material or piece contributes to the overall picture. Here, a combination of limestone, warm wood, and modern appliances work in harmony. The countertops are Gascogne Grey limestone, and the backsplash is a 6-by-6-inch Moroccan tile from Mosaic House. The floors are beautiful warm antique chestnut, and hardware is an antique pewter finish. I liked the contrast of an aged patina here.

This homeowner loves to cook, so we selected a Caliber Indoor Professional range that has high-output burners. This range is not for the casual cook. It's a serious range that you must learn how to use. One reason I chose it is the owner of the company personally inspects and cares for it, so if anything goes wrong, he is a phone call away. Cooking with steam is now a part of most kitchens, and a Miele combination steam oven is a top choice. To have an oven that bakes, broils, roasts, and injects a certain amount of steam will give you a moist meal that is crispy and brown as well. The unit can also accommodate sous vide cooking, which is cooking at a controlled temperature in a bag immersed in hot water to cook slowly. These are not your mother's appliances!

The fridge on the tall wall is a fully concealed Sub-Zero, and a small under-counter freezer is for ice and ice-cream. The laundry room has a large second refrigerator and freezer that accommodates all the surplus food and beverages unit. It is very important to balance the amount of refrigeration and freezer space in a home. There is no need for a tall freezer to take up prime real estate in the kitchen. Keep the space in the kitchen for the items you use every day, and the large freezer in the laundry area, or where there is plenty of room, for long-term freezer storage. A thoughtfully orchestrated kitchen, like this beautiful home, is always a balance between how it looks and how it works.

—Majestic Hudson River Valley—

SPANISH RENAISSANCE | IRVINGTON, NEW YORK

Hudson Valley has many magnificent private landmark homes, aside from the 28 public historic estates, which anyone interested in classical architecture should visit. In the first decade of the twentieth century, a man by the name of Daniel Bacon made a wisely groundbreaking, yet unconventional architectural decision. After growing weary of the grand homes destroyed by fire or torn down, he commissioned architect Oswald C. Hering to design a reinforced-concrete home in the Spanish Renaissance style.

Concrete provided a fireproof, damp-proof foundation for the home, and a concrete home would also be protected from potential repairs, liberating Bacon from insurance and maintenance. The only wood item was to be the roof rafters, which he had covered in tile. Today the house still stands strong.

I was speechless upon arriving at this Spanish Renaissance home. The astounding level of historic preservation took my breath away. The exterior was intact in the same style as it had been developed a century ago, as well as most of the interior.

Sadly, the kitchen had been remodeled sometime in the 1990s and consequentially stripped of any historical architectural elements that it once embodied. The back staircase was removed and replaced with brushed aluminum square balusters. The fireplace surround was replaced with an Italianate-style mantle that curved out into the room with an 18-inch projection. The depth of the mantle pushed the eating table off axis to the rest of the room, denying the possibility for any storage.

Fortunately, most of the existing Sheetrock beams were not structural and could be removed. I wanted to return the ceiling and the surrounding beams to the original aesthetic. The 1990s kitchen had no character and no connection with the architectural features that are an integral part of this home.

The kitchen space is long and narrow. We removed the existing sink that sat under the front window, which we replaced with a larger, lower window, like the original. It brings symmetry to the front of the home and fits seamlessly as it is designed to match the

existing window. French doors were added where the refrigerator once lived to bring in more natural light, as do mirrors at the opposite end. The doors exit to the terrace and are a mirror image of the entry to the outdoor porch.

While aesthetically on par with our ideation of the space, I had to configure a way to ensure these beneficial architectural changes would make this kitchen functional for a family of four. The room presented substantial challenges to this objective. With little to no storage and nowhere to expand, I had to utilize every viable inch of space.

I extended the kitchen into the breakfast room, and in doing so, I took advantage of the different options of appliances. I moved the fully concealed Sub-Zero refrigerator and freezer units over to the window seat, still easily accessible from the work area. In removing the old fireplace surround, I carefully selected a new one that had minimum projection so that the eating table could be moved toward the center of the room. Not only did the new adjustments coincide spatially, but extending into the eating area elongated the appearance of the kitchen and made it feel more spacious.

Hoods are always a marvelous focal point. I can tell what materials a hood should be by the age and character of the home. This finely detailed copper hood with brass trim was inspired by an old copper hood I had viewed in a European castle.

I was able to maximize every bit of storage space through meticulous planning. Pantry storage and appliance storage are to either side of the windows seats. With minimal drawer space by the range, I opted to provide other alternatives for spice storage and instead utilize these drawers for utensils. I methodically planned how this space would be used for the highest livable functionality possible. The 7-inch-deep cabinet between the new window and French door to the terrace holds an abundance of food snacks, teas, and coffees.

Pro Tips
Get creative with storage ideas

Window seats with drawers beneath them are perfect perfect for storing linens, small appliances, outdoor plates, and glasses for the terrace, or even toys for youngsters.

Roll-out shelves in a tall cabinet are useful to store small appliances.

Vertical pull-outs flanking the oven are a convenient place to store oils, herbs, and spices that are used often. Ovens are well insulated today and do not cause a heat problem.

Capture shallow storage wherever you can. It is very useful for jars, canned goods, teas, glasses, and more.

A bookshelf, as simple as it may seem, is a sure way of adding storage and a pop of color and could be located most anywhere in a kitchen.

Due to the new French doors and window, the room receives a robust stream of light, and the staircase is returned to the original aesthetic. I spent a lot of time measuring the front entry staircase to perfectly capture the simple yet refined details to match. The ceiling beams now carry the same aesthetic as the beams in the front of the house. I designed storage for every possible wall that I could, including two tall pantries flanking the fireplace. They house dishes, glasses, and so much more, and the antique mirror doors create a larger impression of space. I must admit, I never thought I would see an empty shelf in this home.

We were lucky that the space where the butler's pantry once was still existed. During my tour of the home the strong presence of the quarter-sawn white-oak doors and trim stood out, leading me to believe that the once very beautiful butler's pantry needed to be redesigned respecting the home's aesthetic. The sliding glass doors are reminiscent of pantries from decades ago. The fully concealed appliances provide modern amenities and yet the feeling of age is restored.

Though faced with numerous obstacles and restraints, we succeeded in making a beautiful, working kitchen for this family of four, and the space embodies the architectural integrity originally intentioned a century ago.

Bridging the Past and Future

TUDOR | BRONXVILLE, NEW YORK

Charles Lewis Bowman designed this wonderful house in the vernacular Tudor style in the early 1900s. Wanting to renovate the interior, the owners engaged Douglas C. Wright Architects and interior designer Brian J McCarthy, Inc, and I was delighted when Douglas called me for my kitchen expertise. I feel honored and excited to work on these magnificent historical homes, respecting and preserving their architectural integrity and character. Doing so presents challenges, yet offers the unique opportunity to reimagine a classic structure.

British architect Sir Edwin Lutyens inspired Bowman, and one can see the influence throughout. Being of the Tudor style, the original kitchen was relegated to the back-of-house where it appeared small, dark, and uninspired. The low ceiling and awkward shape made it drab and impractical, and over-designed pantries with pull-outs and swivel shelves, installed during a 1990s remodel, meant there wasn't enough space to properly store things away. The room did, however, have beautiful architecture. Leaded windows and a gorgeous circular staircase (my favorite stair) offered the potential to craft a redeeming design with improved function. The finished kitchen would have to respect the original architecture while better suiting the needs of the client and family.

Douglas and Brian completely renovated and designed the interiors, but they wanted a specialist designer to address the kitchen and pantry. An addition for a home such as this is out of the question, so a kitchen for a modern family lifestyle must be reconfigured within the existing space. This kitchen is where the client's three children eat, snack, and do their homework, and where their extended family cooks and gathers during the holidays. As such, it needed much better light, space, and flow to be spacious and comfortable for spending time together. By removing the walls between the kitchen, pantry, and stair, we created one large and unified space that would become the hub of the home for this very active family. As much as I love a separate charming old pantry, there are times you must compromise to find space.

Calacatta countertops and quarter-sawn oak cabinetry with cerused finish transformed the room into a light and welcoming space. These features provided a passage to improving the atmosphere while adopting historical design components. Brian chose the most fabulous textured metal backsplash, which has a reflective quality that also enhances the light in the room. I based the profile of the millwork and the hammered pulls, knobs, and olive-knuckle hinges on the architectural detailing in the front of the house, continuing Bowman's aesthetic intent into the kitchen. Sometimes the best source of inspiration resides in existing elements of the house.

Every inch of space counted in this room, and nowhere more so than in the pantry. By carefully calculating the proportions of windows, cabinetry, and backsplash, I increased storage area and created a sense of verticality for greater height. We lowered the bottom of the window to the countertop and installed a 14-inch-high backsplash—shorter than the 18-inch-high backsplash in the kitchen—that enables the wall cabinets to be taller, feel more prominent, and provide better storage. The beautiful leaded windows are replicated in the cabinet doors, reflecting light and giving a more formal appearance.

This kitchen is designed with two comprehensive workstations so the client and her mother can comfortably cook at the same time. Removing the wall of the butler's pantry was necessary to have a central island, and the newly found space permitted the island workstation to have an easy flow around it. The prep sink in the island allows for interaction with the children while seated at the curved countertop. This placement is conveniently located in front of the range as well. Another large sink in front of the leaded windows is the primary cleaning area. This means one can use the clean-up station, while someone else preps, and never get in each other's way. The fully concealed refrigerator and freezer are off to the side in a common area, and easy to get to from either sink.

Numerous pots can fit on the 48-inch range when the family cooks their fine Italian cuisine—I can smell their delicious tomato sauce now! They also have a steam oven and high-speed combination oven. A steam oven should be a part of every kitchen today, and high-speed combination ovens are also of great benefit for busy households. Cooking a chicken in half the time comes in handy when you arrive home late in the day from after-school activities.

This kitchen required a delicate balance of beauty and function. It needed to work within the confines of an existing space in a superb home, and to be reimagined for the client's day-to-day living needs. The kitchen now provides more storage and functionality, and feels more welcoming, bright, and uplifting. The space can fulfill the necessary duties of the room while offering an atmosphere that draws people in and invites them to stay awhile. The apparent effortlessness of the room belies the complexity of its planning, but the meticulous process resulted in such immense value for the client, and for myself to have contributed to this impressive historical home.

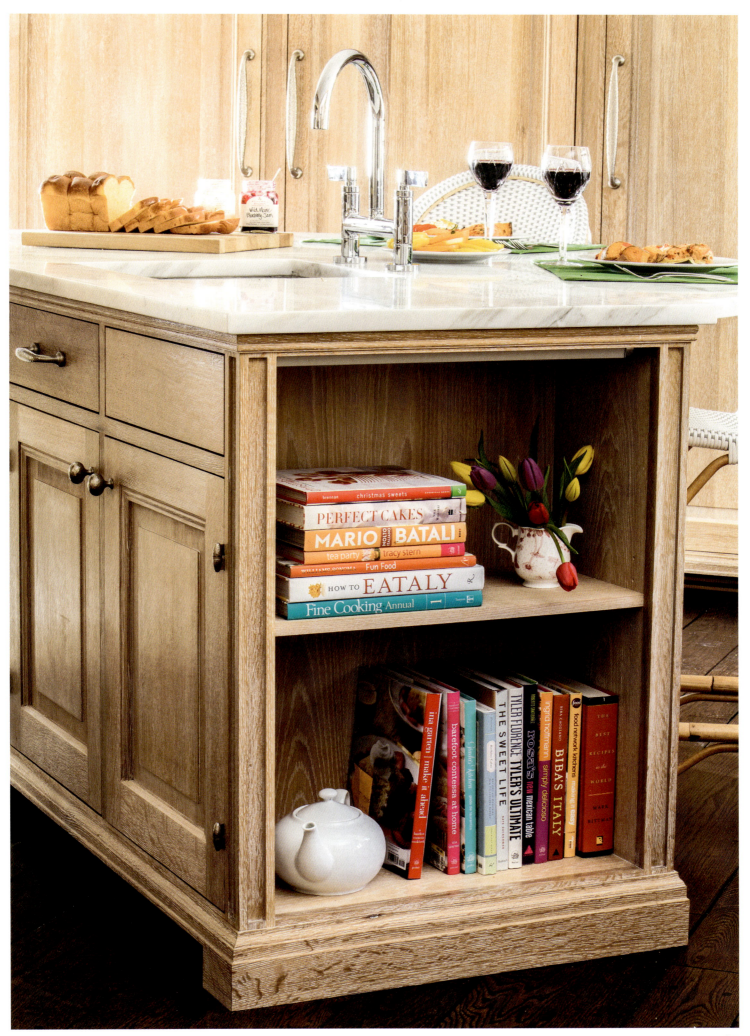

Pro Tips

Lighten and brighten a dark room

Older homes notoriously have lower ceilings. Consider a lower height backsplash—16 inches versus 18 inches—wherever you can. A tall cabinet or taller wall cabinet will provide a feeling of added height, and the lower backsplash allows the first and second shelf of the wall cabinet to be lower for easy accessibility.

Removing walls, wherever possible, will create a more open and generous area. However, respecting the historical integrity of a home is equally important, so ensure the removal of walls does not compromise the classic architectural foundation, or reduce necessary storage. Make sure you design an alternate location for storage capacity.

Larger windows will let more natural light inside, and reflective materials will bounce light into the room. Antique mirrors will also enliven a space with light and character, giving the illusion of an expansion of the space.

Surface-mounted and pendant fixtures should be the dominant form of lighting in a kitchen, in addition to natural light. They maintain character, scale, and proportion within every room they are installed.

—A Special Place in Bedford—

SCOTTISH BARONIAL | BEDFORD, NEW YORK

That age-old saying "don't mix business with pleasure" leaps to mind when I think about this kitchen and pantry in Bedford, New York. It started as a business venture, but it was such a pleasure to design that it evolved into a great bond between myself and the clients. They have become very dear friends, and I know the kitchen has stood the test of time because we cook together every holiday. I am always quick to tease them, asking who designed their wonderful and beautifully functional kitchen and pantry. The effort expended in creating this kitchen was exponentially redeemed. I am so thrilled to have made a special place for people who are dear to me, and the memories they make in this room every day.

With three active young children, the homeowners wanted an addition for a new kitchen and family room. The house is a stone Scottish Baronial built in 1905, with the kitchen remodeled in the 1980s. The laminate Formica left a lot to be desired, as did the functionality, which was not up to modern standards. Transforming the kitchen in a design faithful to the architecture would be both daunting and exciting. My goal was to create an area that would accommodate the whole family spatially, aesthetically, and practically. Any architectural additions would have to justly mirror or complement the period attributes of the current arrangement. I set out to ensure the kitchen remodel would be reminiscent of the rest of the home by embracing early twentieth-century influences.

This represents a core tenet of my design beliefs: that the kitchen be integrated into the architecture. Many homes have showstopper kitchens that are not aligned with the architecture of the house, which compromises the overall design effect. Accomplishing this balance, while making the finished product appear seamless, takes an immense amount of work. The challenge here called for a vast array of new elements to resemble or work in tandem with the existing styles and structures.

Our team, which was headed by architect Richard Sammons of Fairfax & Sammons and interior designer Sam Blount, was phenomenal and collaborative. Working alongside professionals who share my dedication to the integrity of the original structure created an ideal foundation for the project. As a classical architect, Richard respected the architectural style and carried the aesthetic through to the new addition. He designed a lovely barrel-vaulted ceiling framed with a paneled entablature, and the mahogany leaded glass windows are in keeping with the front of the house. The rolled-up screen in the window frames is one of my favorite details. I love it when these are incorporated, as you're not looking out a screen when they are not in use.

The architecture facilitated my work by providing the design's canvas. I naturally understood through this framework what the house wanted to become and what the kitchen needed to be to fit this scheme. As beautiful as this kitchen is, it remains understated in comparison to the rest of the house. Yes, it is still the back-of-house, even though families use their kitchens today more than ever.

The kitchen addition includes a full wall of paneled windows that illuminate the space with natural light. The crisp contrast between the light millwork and dark countertops is timelessly elegant while simultaneously cheering and welcoming. Stainless-steel appliances create that transition between traditional comfort and modern utility.

The millwork is integrated into the architecture, flowing from the mudroom to the kitchen, then onto the wet bar and family room. Each opening has an integrated paneled jamb delineating each space, yet concurrently tying them together to create a sense of unity. All spaces possess unique qualities while remaining true to the original foundation of the house. Rather than the new addition appearing as a separate entity, its style integrates the new space into the preexisting rooms with ease.

At the far end of the kitchen lies another set of paneled windows that overlook the view from the front of the house. A desk is nestled into the nook with a lovely paneled jamb indicating a break from where the kitchen ends and the desk begins. The jamb reaches around both sides of the desk to create the perfect space for bookshelves, tucked neatly into an alcove on each side.

The cabinetry millwork is designed like furniture, incorporating little feet in front of the recessed kickboard for the illusion of being raised off the floor. This structure allows the space to appear to physically elevate—it is more decorative than having just the kickboard, and it anchors the cabinetry in the room. Each piece of cabinetry becomes independent from one another to feel less bulky.

With its neutral color palette, this kitchen will never go out of date. It's classic, simple, and timeless. I love the naïveté of a V-groove backsplash, which emits enough character without overwhelming the other kitchen elements. The soapstone countertops develop a wonderful patina over time. Each aspect of a kitchen design should be thoughtfully considered as to how it will fare. As this family grows, the kitchen will capture countless memories, reflected in how its character adapts over time. Designs should have room to evolve, with strong enough foundations to maintain integrity to the original model. That's where this soapstone excels as well. It is very forgiving and may be freshened up with mineral oil if scratched.

This kitchen accommodates a lot of appliances—I have never had to fit in more! A warming oven, high-speed electric oven, refrigerator drawers, and full refrigerator are along one wall, and a 36-inch range and a 24-inch range on the opposite wall. The kitchen island has a set of freezer drawers, and there is a dishwasher to each side of the sink—one for everyday use and one for entertaining. The larger freezer is positioned in the larder outside this room. These additions exemplify the ability to incorporate utility

Pro Tips

Beauty and functionality coexist in the kitchen

Prioritizing utility does not mean beauty must be sacrificed. The two can coexist with enough foresight and ambition. Aesthetic goals can be met and surpassed, even in a kitchen packed with hefty, functional appliances.

Invest in materials that will beautify over time. Soapstone is a durable countertop that develops a stunning patina, and gains character as more memories are made, and far outweighs countertop materials that will eventually break or wear down unattractively.

Cabinetry designed to resemble furniture, with small feet in front of the recessed kickboard, creates a more finished look, much like the baseboard around a room. This is more decorative than having just the kickboard, and it elevates the aesthetic and character of the space.

Protect any wood paneling around the sink with a low backsplash in the same material as the countertop, such as soapstone. This will create a seamlessness and ensure the wood is preserved.

pieces in an aesthetic setting. Fitting in each appliance can seem daunting, but it creates an opportunity to accomplish two goals when designing a kitchen: function and beauty. The kitchen is often regarded as a room of function, but this does not mean beauty needs to be sacrificed in the process of fulfilling this purpose. Being proud of the aesthetics of a space should be on par with the desire to maximize utility.

For inspiration to design the butler's pantry—a collaboration with the Fairfax & Sammons team, along with my constant study of McKim, Mead & White butler's pantries—I looked at Ogden Mills's mansion in Staatsburgh, New York. Homes like these are known for their fine millwork, and I wanted to capitalize on the abundant details, such as the sliding glass pantry doors, which were a signature detail of Stanford White.

The pantry has gorgeous leathered absolute black countertops, white oak millwork, and sliding glass cabinet doors. Brackets support the wall cabinets, and a framing bead runs up the vertical edge of the doors in a traditional fashion. I continued the wood in the backsplash panels yet protected the base of it with granite. This family owns an extensive wine collection, and the cupboard heights and depths are custom designed to fit the various dimensions of their wine glasses comfortably.

I embarked on this project with the objective of giving a family an appealing kitchen and pantry that would capture the full potential of the space for their needs. Seeing how they have grown into this kitchen reinforces my core design values of beauty and utility in harmony, and their enjoyment of this space undoubtedly stands as the most redeeming quality.

This kitchen represents the fruits of a wonderful, synergetic team that understands and appreciates classical architecture. Our unified goals and visions paved the way to an incredible outcome. While Richard, Sam, and I had different responsibilities, the merging of our concentrated efforts resulted in an interconnected final product. The integration of millwork into the architecture reads and functions as one cohesive and beautiful space.

Mediterranean in Connecticut

SPANISH REVIVAL | DARIEN, CONNECTICUT

This fabulous Spanish Revival house designed by Wesley Sherwood Bessell was built in the 1930s as the summer residence for the famous pianist and composer Frank La Forge. Perched on the banks of tranquil Gorham's Pond in Darien, Connecticut, the house is grand, as was customary of that era. That grandness, however, never reached the back-of-house. The kitchen, no larger than a butler's pantry, had been designed as a service kitchen and lacked the space and amenities needed by the homeowner—a talented gourmet chef.

The client engaged me to design a new kitchen, but it would require an extension that respected the Mediterranean aesthetic of the house. I recommended my long-time collaborator Sheldon Richard Kostelecky Architect for the occasion. Sheldon is as passionate about classical architecture as I am, and he designed an addition with stunning architectural elements that the house so profoundly deserved.

The addition is subservient to the original house, residing on a lower plane than the rest of the building. This position allows for a wide sweeping view of the grounds and pond. The garage and entry are on the first floor, and a staircase leads up to the new kitchen and a three-season outdoor terrace. Limestone flooring, plain stucco walls, and ceiling beams salvaged from old Connecticut barns continue the interior aesthetic of the original house. The Spanish-style corner fireplace, glass French doors, and triple arch windows are modeled after others in the home.

This set the stage for us to design a kitchen that met my client's needs, embraced the Mediterranean architectural language, and flowed beautifully from the home. Creating a kitchen in this room was a pleasure. It was so architecturally correct, with lines from the entry through to the screened porch. Influence presented itself copiously in the home's rich history, surrounding outdoor views, and architectural style. It was an inspiring challenge and enthralling feat to bring it all together.

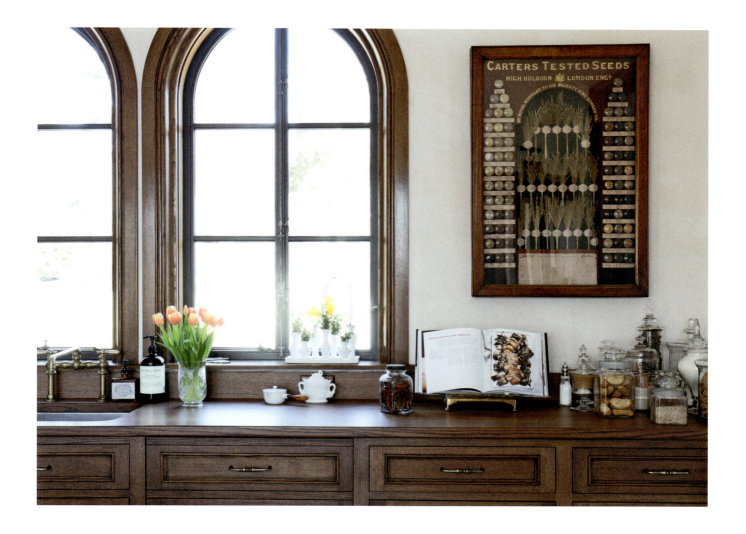

Working with the symmetrical layout of the room, we placed the owner's 11-foot-long antique glass-front cabinet and claret-red AGA cooker on opposing walls. Both draw enough intrigue individually, while still contributing to the cohesiveness of the general aesthetic. Each is flanked by openings, with the glass doors next to the AGA cooker leading out to the terrace where a Kalamazoo Rotisserie is situated. A stucco-covered hood above the cooker is trimmed with beams, and integrated into the architecture of the room.

Never be fearful of incorporating furniture such as this beautiful china cabinet into a kitchen design. It adds character and is extremely functional. Many times, we will outfit the interior with roll outs or additional shelves. We often will take out the utensil drawers.

The long continuous countertop and sink are along the rear wall, offering a view out of three arched windows, while the island in the center has a view across the breakfast table to the outdoors and pond. Extending the countertop from wall-to-wall provides plenty of workspace along with the island. There are no wall cabinets, keeping the kitchen light and open and accentuating its architectural language. This provides the decorative ceiling beams with their fair share of attention, as well as the long, intricate chandelier.

I love a kitchen island that offers more than just the traditional island. This island was modeled from the island table in my own American Farmhouse home (featured at the end of this book). Drawers on each side, with a diamond detail on the reclaimed oak millwork, provide plenty of storage space for utensils and cookware. An open shelf allows pots and pans to be on view, and a custom slit in the honed Carrara marble countertop means the owner's favorite knives are always within easy reach. Of course, this is not for every home, but can provide a unique detail for the serious chef.

The dark wood countertop beneath the arched windows adheres to the aesthetic of the original kitchen, as does the double sink, which originated from the service kitchen. The Monel composition of the sink reflects the age of the house. Monel is a nickel-copper alloy that preceded stainless steel, and was even used on the magnificent Chrysler Building. The beautiful sink deserved to be restored. My metal fabricator reinforced the sink and we complemented it with two sets of traditional-style faucets.

Because this kitchen has no wall cabinets, its functionality depends upon supporting rooms for integrating the appliances and storage. The refrigerator, ovens, and small appliances are in an adjacent vestibule where they can be easily accessed but are out of sight. Designating bulky pieces to neighboring spaces allows for more room to work within the actual kitchen and keeps the dining areas feeling airy and pleasant. The old kitchen is the other side of this small room. In there is a large pantry for food storage, and the original cast-iron and ceramic-tiled cabinet doors, which retain the Spanish Revival character of the house.

By respecting the architectural language, this new kitchen feels as if it was always there, even after being constructed ninety years after the house was built. Not only does it fit aesthetically, but now offers the space and amenities a gourmet chef needs. Through mimicking classical design properties, this kitchen perfectly encapsulates the era and style of the original, while offering facilities for modern use.

Pro Tips

Unique pieces and details add character and charm

Unique pieces, antiques, and heirlooms can set the stage in a modern or traditional kitchen. They provide warmth, character, and charm, and are wonderful conversation starters.

Antique sinks are beautiful. Most of these old sinks are made of Monel, which is very durable and can last for many more years if looked after. Check the sink seams and make sure they will hold up. Ask a local metal fabricator to ensure there are no leaks, and have a specialist reseal seams.

AGA ranges also can add great character to a kitchen. They add age and warmth and are very user friendly. The original gas version is on all the time and should be turned off during the summer months. Or integrate AGA's more modern unit that can be turned off after use.

A slit in your countertop for knives is a great look and incredibly functional. Be advised this is not recommended for every kitchen, especially if children are around.

Consider detail on the ceiling, whether it is beams, wood boards, or a coffer detail. This finishes the room.

A Classic Beauty

CLASSICAL | SCARSDALE, NEW YORK

One of the fundamental attributes of classical architecture and design is its holistic nature. Classicism is not a style, it's a set of rules and principles that one abides by. All parts are integral to creating a cohesive whole. You must consider every feature prevalent to a design to complete the space. This kitchen, though classic and restrained, contains endless detailing inspired by the rest of the house. My ultimate resource library on any excellent design is to walk through a historic, classical home such as this.

This house was built in the 1910s, although the kitchen had been remodeled around 2004, before the client purchased the home. The architecture had good bones and the kitchen was beautiful. However, it was not well-built or functional for the family, and the level of quality was not on par with the home. The clients are very bright and philanthropic people with a deep respect for history. They were such a pleasure to work with as they understood and appreciated the delicate details of my work.

I spent an immense amount of time analyzing the proportions and details for this millwork, including the interior doors, rails, and drawers. With its recessed panel and slight rise in the center, the door detail is reminiscent of that in the front of the house. The crown detail is also a replica of the molding in the original house. The historic plantation home Battersea in St Petersburg, Virginia, inspired the pilaster detail on the cabinet tiles. It has a recess with a softly raised radius inside—a detail I adore.

As the size of the room was fixed, I had to work within the given space to create balance, functionality, and symmetry throughout. Cabinetry flanks the door that leads to the front foyer, and separating the specialized wall ovens provides a far more attractive design with symmetry on both sides. The wall cabinets, base cabinets, and appliances align with those on the opposite wall. Excluding top drawers on the base cabinets achieved simplicity and verticality. A full-height base door with a bank of adjacent drawers provides a cleaner aesthetic. The offset pivot hinge—one of my favorites—is prevalent in fine furniture and provides a clean look while being barely visible.

The range, refrigerator, and sink are close to one another to create a triangle of key work areas. The clean-up sink is by the window, and the prep sink is in the island. It has a linear pitched drain carved into the countertop to create a drainboard flowing into the sink. Ample wall storage for dishes and the dishwasher are right nearby, so anyone could work at the clean-up station and not interfere with others working in the kitchen simultaneously.

The solid-glass painted backsplash is in a custom color and installed in sheets. The aesthetic is as clean as it gets while maintaining a timeless feel. The sleek lines and curved back of the Nanz drawer handle are also timeless and modern, and much easier to grasp than a stylized drawer head. The light-colored quartzite countertop has beautiful variation in tone and veining.

We installed a large, professional, residential Sub-Zero refrigerator as we were swayed by the vast amount of functions and the accuracy of the cooling. Designing can be a juggle and a balance, and secondary items that can be appropriately installed in an ancillary room should be. In this case, a large refrigerator and freezer from the existing kitchen needed a spot. After careful study of adjacent back-of-house rooms, I installed them in a mudroom closet just off the kitchen. This allowed for more flexibility and avoided an unsightly mass of appliances in the kitchen itself.

The clients expressed their desire to keep their countertop-height dining table in the kitchen, as they enjoyed sitting here for family meals. We made the dining table with a stone top that abuts the kitchen island to appear as one piece. This hybrid counter-table creates a multifunctional work and dining surface. Surface-mounted lights and pendants overhead resemble the traditional architecture of the house. They also expel a more robust light than a directional recess light.

Historical inspiration was the driving force behind designing the butler's pantry. All millwork comes from research inspired by the history of this home, Battersea, and McKim, Mead & White houses. The cabinetry is stained tiger maple with sliding glass-front doors. The ratchet system within the cupboards is reminiscent of how these shelves were installed in decades past, which uses supports to hold the shelving in place. The unlacquered brass Hamilton Sinkler hardware and the warmth of the wood prepare you for a transition to the more formal dining room.

An inlet marked by a picturesque oval window provided a staging area for food when entertaining. A specified staging area is essential for a buffet, as it provides a setting for food, or a coffee and aperitif after a meal. Since this butler's pantry serves as a wet bar, this ancillary area bridges the pantry and family room to the kitchen. The color scheme of this area matched that of the kitchen more closely, with similar colored millwork and overhead shelves. The symmetry along the wall coupled with the statement window creates a pleasing, almost soothing effect.

Pro Tips

Choose strong, durable, long-lasting countertops

Kitchens are one of the most-used spaces in a house and the materials, especially countertops, need to withstand wear and tear while maintaining their good looks.

Quartzite and sintered stone are strong and durable options. They hold their own against stains, while maintaining the chic look of light-colored stone. Quartzite is a hard, dense, naturally occurring stone that will withstand day-to-day abuse. A quartzite can be honed, polished, or leathered, each providing a very different look. The quartzite countertop in this kitchen has beautiful variation in tone and veining. Quartz (different from quartzite) is an engineered manmade product created from crushed stone and a small percentage of resins. Sintered stone is also engineered, but it is composed of all natural minerals and stone particles. If the budget allows, I steer clients toward quartzite or sintered stone as they are extremely practical and durable.

Marble is the best surface to roll out your cookie dough. However marble, like limestone, is not resilient enough to staining and scratching. A quality sealer is always recommended on any stone, especially marble.

A year and a half after completing the kitchen, the client called me to design their master bathroom. Once again, the architecture had good bones. A wonderful glory-vaulted ceiling, decorative tiled floor, and symmetrical layout set the stage. However, the room didn't function well and needed to be designed holistically.

The vanity and dressing table face opposite walls, with their mirrors creating a kaleidoscopic effect. You would never know all the mirrors are very discreet medicine cabinets. The cabinets didn't need a lot of depth, so integrating them into the design was an easier endeavor. I designed the drawer handles and knobs with gnarling, and the cylindrical Nanz paumelle hinge is very pure and simplistic. It's a design taken from the nineteenth-century and stripped of all superfluous ornament. The decorative hardware contributes just enough contrast, and the mosaic marble floor adds a bold pattern to the white background.

The bathtub occupies prime position, bathed in light in front of the windows. The water closet and the shower are surrounded by etched glass walls to provide privacy and receive ample sunlight. They demonstrate a way to build a wall in a tight space without compromising any architectural trim. The symmetrical placement wasn't in the existing design, and there wasn't enough width to insert walls for casing around the window. Instead of a standard wall, I used a pane of etched glass, which is thinner and lets light into the water closet and shower while still offering privacy. The slim width of the glass walls meant I could control the symmetry of the room and put full casing around the window. The shower floor is a solid slab of Bardiglio marble so that it doesn't require grout. It's pitched with a lineal drain and honed to create texture for grip.

Designing multiple rooms within this home allowed me to unify different areas through similar attributes. Themes of symmetry and dedication to historical influence ring vibrantly throughout the whole. As the parts of each individual project come together, they build a calming sense of unity, even when these spaces have completely different purposes. Seeing the conclusion of the finished product becomes all the more gratifying after adhering to the same rules and principles in each individual space.

Family Memories and Traditions

NEW ENGLAND FARMHOUSE | SHARON, CONNECTICUT

The renovation of this 1830s farmhouse in Sharon, Connecticut, was a labor of love and truly rewarding. The owners purchased the house in 1986. They raised their son there, and the walls hold an abundance of sentimental memories for the family. So when the owner called me after a fire ravaged the home in 2010, I was deeply moved, and elated to be able to lend my design expertise. I was already familiar with the family, as I had designed the kitchen in their Manhattan apartment. For this endeavor, I understood the sensitivity needed for the restoration and remodel of the historical house. They wanted a home reminiscent enough of the original to retain their important memories, while being functional and comfortable for decades to come.

The house and the owners' memorabilia had been severely damaged by smoke and water during the fire, saved only by the lath and plaster walls of the farmhouse. The scope of the project extended beyond the kitchen into the entire home, and we restored the house with a sympathetic renovation and an addition that brought it into the current day.

Inspections of the extensive damage and aged structural framing required the house to be brought up to code. We shelled the interior of the house to rebuild the framework, leaving the exterior intact. The original 12-over-12 windows and doors were reused with restoration glass to match the original, and we incorporated the dismantled chestnut framing and half-log rafters into the decorative design of some rooms. Repurposing viable fragments gave new life to dated yet attractive materials.

The farmhouse is the nineteenth-century New England vernacular of "big house, little house, back house, barn," with the little house being an ell. The existing kitchen located in the ell was small, but now I had the opportunity to create a larger, modern kitchen for the homeowners who love to cook and entertain. The design had dual obligations: to fit the clients' lifestyle and the classic structure of the house. To achieve this, I kept the design understated, befitting the farmhouse style and aesthetic.

The lath and plaster walls are left unpainted, expressing their beautiful waxed finish. Simple cabinetry with a lip detail is painted "Mouse's Back" by Farrow & Ball, softening the transition from the pale plaster to the weathered black granite countertops. These colors and materials create a calming palette with just enough contrast to add character. The standing-seam metal rangehood was custom made, as was the wrought-iron hardware. The appliances are masked behind the cabinet fronts, and there are minimal wall cabinets to enhance the light and create a greater sense of height in the room.

The owner wanted a fireplace in the kitchen. I felt it only natural to design and build a Rumford fireplace in keeping with those in other rooms of the house, with the added bonus that this type of fireplace forces heat into the room. The fire provides beautiful warmth in the winter as the back wall is pitched, and the soapstone surround and hearth have a softly textured finish. The pantry, off the kitchen, has been built as per the original house, and a new basement with a wine cellar has the original chestnut subflooring on its walls.

Pro Tips

Patinated materials imbue age and warmth

Dark, textured, and salvaged materials can instill a sense of time and character in any kitchen. They should be used strategically and purposefully for a considered aesthetic.

When selecting black countertops, honed material will show marks from fingerprints, oil, and anything else that touches it. Consider a leather finish instead, such as leathered black absolute countertops. Its subtle texture hides a multitude of unattractive blemishes.

Repurposed beams, framing, and boards from a dismantled barn can achieve a warm and relaxed aesthetic and charm for any home, new or old. If one cannot salvage these materials from their own home, look for a local supplier.

Plaster-on-lath walls with a waxed finish have a beautiful, natural look with a subtle texture. Waxing plaster walls means they can be washed while also providing durability. Plus, plaster is a non-combustible material.

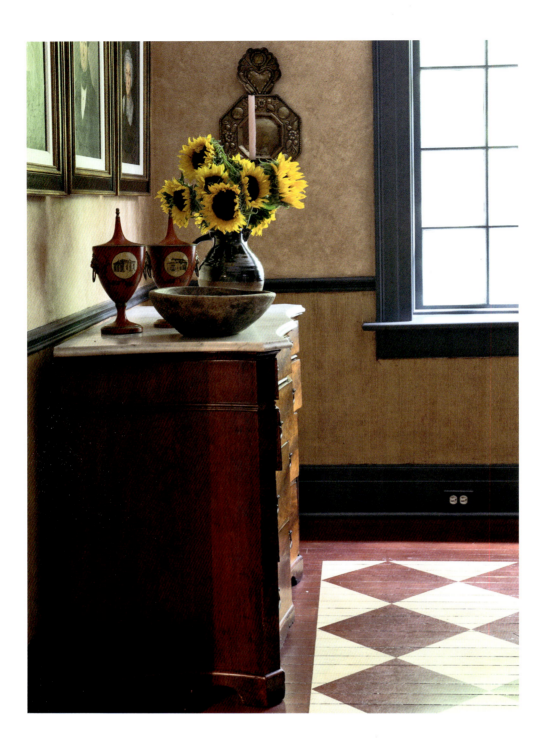

Next to the kitchen, the dining room has a painted floor with a checkerboard red and white. Painted wood floors are a way to bring in color and pattern in lieu of a rug, and to salvage damaged old floors that cannot be re-sanded. Along with the natural aged boards, the color and effect are a perfect complement to the faux hand-painted plaster walls.

The fire originated in the study, thus it needed extensive restoration work. We redid the millwork, retained the hearth, reproduced the fireplace surround, and widened all the doorways.

126   CLASSIC KITCHENS FOR MODERN LIVING

With the son soon heading off to college at the time of the build, I wanted to provide additional bedroom and bathroom space for the family to have more privacy and comfort. There had only been one small bathroom added to this farmhouse and it serviced three bedrooms. We added a second story to the ell, creating a master bedroom suite with a master bathroom and dressing room. The dismantled chestnut framing now lines the ceiling as charming rafters, and a Rumford fireplace fills the room with a golden glow. The once small bathroom on the second floor was removed to open up the hallway, and a former bedroom was converted into a larger bathroom for their son and other guests.

The owners named their newly renovated house Colinwood, in honor of their son and the memories it embodies. It will always be their home, through tranquility and turmoil. Now Colinwood offers twenty-first-century necessities but retains its nineteenth-century farmhouse charm. The renovation demonstrates how distress can find a grand new chapter with proper attention and application.

FAMILY MEMORIES AND TRADITIONS 131

Transformed and Treasured

COLONIAL | DARIEN, CONNECTICUT

I have a wonderful clientele and the reward of working with such fabulous people means more to me than anything. I loved the collaboration with this couple who appreciate quality and care about the process required to achieve the result. We spent a great deal of time laying out their kitchen so that it flows well, works for their specific needs, and is extremely functional with everything having its place. The client had inherited an extensive collection of antiques from his mother, so we created a classic, timeless, and subdued space in which the treasured pieces would resonate.

There is a real methodology in laying out a kitchen. It doesn't matter how small or grand the kitchen is, it must function well. When I collaborate with a client, I extrapolate how they live and like to work in their kitchen. Once I understand this, I can break the layout down into different components and then put them together logically and in relationship to each other.

Every kitchen has a primary, secondary, and tertiary countertop, and each countertop must have a relationship to a sink, refrigerator, or range, otherwise it won't be used. We designated the island with the integrated sink as the primary countertop and positioned the refrigerator, freezer, and wall ovens behind it for easy access when prepping, but not to interrupt the active work space. All prep items are stored in the island's cabinetry to make cooking convenient and to reduce the amount of walking around for ease and efficiency. Islands can be a curse if the appliances are not positioned correctly.

The secondary countertop is located between the range and the main sink, where it used for multiple purposes. Produce and other items are cleaned in this sink and then prepared on the counter. Placing this sink directly beneath the outward-facing window makes this preparation a more pleasant duty. Having this counter area is important when multiple workstations are being used simultaneously, so that each person has their own primary station and doesn't interfere with one another.

The tertiary countertop is to the left of the main sink. This countertop is not supported by appliances or a work area, but rather is where dishes are placed prior to washing or loading into the dishwasher. Accordingly, the dishwasher and cutlery drawers are under this countertop, and the wall cabinets for dishes and glasses are above.

In addition to layout, I pay considerable attention to how appliances look together; how a wall of appliances and cabinetry reads visually. When we embarked on this kitchen, the cooktop was located on the island and the refrigerator on the wall that now houses the range. This was a less-than-ideal aesthetic choice. Now, the wall behind the island prep sink is brimming with appliances but the elevation reads beautifully. A combination-steam and high-speed oven flank the freezer, refrigerator, and pantry, which are behind tall doors, and glass-front cabinets frame the top and sides. It is symmetrical and balanced, and the proportions are well thought through. Appliances available today can be fully integrated, allowing for a plethora of design possibilities. They enable the space to retain extreme functionality while being cohesive and beautiful.

White millwork and quartzite countertop and backsplash are the two materials that make up the space. A classic profile on the millwork accentuates the verticality of the cabinetry, which is needed when working with 8-foot-high ceilings. It adds a sense of height to the room, and the simplicity of the quartzite backsplash is a clean and elegant look.

The entablature around the perimeter of the cabinetry and room has a timeless detail that dates back to the Roman Doric order. The cornice, at the top of the entablature, is a functional element on the exterior of many buildings and is used as a finishing detail at the top of a room. I call it decorative punctuation.

Scale is an imperative component when beautifying a kitchen, especially in a space like this where the work was confined to the existing room and the doorway was elected not to be moved. Each part of the kitchen plays a role in the composition. I try to avoid implementing a singular stand-out feature, which typically becomes tired over time. Rather, my approach focuses on creating a sophisticated, refined look that prioritizes longevity, balance, and timelessness. The kitchen is one of the most challenging spaces to maintain an overall sense of coordination because there are so many moving parts, such as appliance sizes, countertop heights, and existing architecture, which often interfere with one another. Working against these conflicting elements is impossible, so I embrace creative solutions to work with them, and allow the individual aspects of the room to be read and evaluated as a whole. Thus scale becomes important in bringing unity and cohesion to the elements. Here, the height of the door and the historical four-step crown detail appear simplistic, yet they maximize the vertical layout of the room.

The client had inherited beautiful antiques from his mother who was an interior designer in New York. We wanted the gorgeous nineteenth-century farmhouse table and delicate birdcage Windsor side chairs to take center stage, so we used a clean white palette for the kitchen to emphasize their beauty. Though this home was a "builder's spec" house, the gorgeous antique pieces add elegance and character and infuse the home with the client's individuality. I find a timeless white room is a good backdrop for accentuating antiques, as the white feels fresh in contrast to the warmth of wood pieces.

The French art moderne eight-light chandelier from Remains Lighting is in keeping with the candelabra that was historically prevalent over a farmhouse table. With simple lines, it hangs modestly above the table. The refined lines and perfect proportions of the Soronson Light Flutes fit the scale of the space. These are the subtle details that allow the eye to enjoy the room, traveling seamlessly from one element to the next. Additionally, the alignment from the pendant light to rangehood elevation is critical to maintaining continuity.

Making a kitchen functional and beautiful requires an abundance of knowledge and detail. The skill is in making it work smoothly and look effortless, and the great reward is in seeing how much the homeowners enjoy it.

Pro Tips

Function and flow are critical in the kitchen

Every kitchen will have its unique challenges, regardless of its size. But flow and function must work together to turn a kitchen into a practical and beautiful room.

Design each workstation (the cooking station, prep station, and clean-up station) to be purposeful and complete, making sure it has autonomous functionality without depending upon other areas. Each station should stand alone and provide all the necessary attributes to guarantee maximal potential usage, or else the kitchen runs the risk of being too busy or inefficient.

Axis lines create harmony in the kitchen. Continuity is key to creating a synchronized space, so ensure planes of sight are consistent throughout the space. Symmetry can help achieve this.

Pathways should not be compromised, and 48-inch-wide walkways are optimal. The wider the walkway and the smaller the island, the larger the kitchen will feel. Islands that are too large overpower the space.

Avoid wraparound corners if possible, as they are not always the best use of space. A straight run is often more efficient and balanced.

French Revival with Flair

FRENCH REVIVAL | DARIEN, CONNECTICUT

I vividly recall the day I was introduced to this project. As I walked into my studio, my staff quietly approached me to say there was a man in the conference room who needed my help. It sounded serious. He told me that he and his wife were downsizing to a new home being built by the water. The architect had designed the kitchen, but his wife was concerned it wouldn't function to its fullest potential. She wanted a kitchen specialist and I had been highly recommended. I agreed and was eager to help.

I met with his extremely talented wife who provided wonderful input throughout the design process. She already had fabulous ideas for the project, and only needed help putting them together and ensuring the kitchen functioned well. We worked very closely together and collaborated with interior decorator Susan Thorn on colors and lighting selections.

The composition of the room took its cues from classic French architecture, with wide-plank floors, timber ceiling beams, and brick walls. When my client approached me with the idea of an antique French fireback, I knew it would be an exquisite focal point behind the range, flanked by the windows and beneath the zinc hood. Our excellent builder cleverly engineered the brick wall to carry the fire shield's hefty weight.

My client also had a cherished collection of majolica china that inspired the color palette for the backsplash. I wanted it to be uniquely special, so we visited Solar Antique Tiles in Manhattan and carefully took some majolica with us. We were greeted with a stunning display of 2-by-2-inch tiles in 27 different shades. Blue, green, yellow, purple, and more. A kaleidoscopic palette that represented every spectrum of the rainbow.

"What color should we choose?" my client asked hesitantly.

"All of them!" I exclaimed.

What fun to have a client who's not afraid to take the plunge with color. The backsplash adds so much character to the kitchen and complements the majolica in the glass-front cabinetry beautifully. The classic white marble countertops selected by Susan accentuate the vibrancy of the backsplash and majolica too. While the soft-gray millwork and zinc island countertop are subdued and understated to visually recede.

I designed the cabinetry to be simpler than was originally presented to me, and to expose the gorgeous timber ceiling beams in their entirety. Meticulous work was necessary to align the top of the crown and window, but that scrupulous detailing is what integrates the kitchen and architecture as a holistically designed room. An excellent builder always helps.

The layout and appliances were just as important as the aesthetic to ensure the kitchen functions successfully while maintaining efficient flow. I developed the kitchen layout using the path of least resistance to minimize the chances of people bumping into one another. (I like to refer to this as "bumper butt.") The sinks, range, and ovens are placed strategically to avoid bottlenecks that would otherwise frustrate the cook. They are configured in, behind, and adjacent to the kitchen island. The refrigerator, pantry, and coffee station are outside of the island and around the perimeter of the room so family and visitors can access them easily without causing a traffic jam.

The clean-up and prep sink next to the range offers a gorgeous view out the window, while the main sink on the kitchen island has an outlook into the magnificent, grand family room. This layout allows my client to chat with friends, family, and grandchildren—the most important of all.

The main thoroughfare separates the island and countertops from a hall of millwork that serves as the pantry, conveniently located next to the breakfast room. These provide storage for dishes as well as a coffee station and a small under-counter refrigerator. This allows for a leisurely breakfast or lunch without getting in the way of the busier kitchen space.

Storage becomes a delicate balance when you downsize. Supporting rooms are as paramount as the kitchen, and every inch of space needs to be programmed. Fortunately, this house had many supporting rooms and closets just outside the kitchen that could be used for this purpose. I commissioned each of the client's items to be categorized and situated: silver, linen, china, crystal, vases, trays, table leaves, and a collection of flavored olive oils. A closet behind the refrigerator wall holds the silver, and the superb food pantry displays the much-loved olive oils.

From the floors to the ceiling, the detailing to the color, my talented client was a pivotal part of designing this project. She has every reason to be proud of the kitchen that she and her family love and enjoy.

Pro Tips

Ensure circulation space for efficient performance

Multiple workstations are a must in a larger kitchen. Consider where and how people might be working and moving in the kitchen, and the possibility that multiple functions will be performed simultaneously. If appliances are crowded in one area, it will create a traffic jam that will frustrate the cook.

If there is one range in a kitchen, choose a multifunctioning unit, and ensure that it has countertop and circulation space around it.

Strategically place the refrigerator, freezer, and pantry away from the immediate workstation to avoid unnecessary bottlenecks.

A tall freezer is considered long-term storage and does not need to be in the kitchen. A small under-counter freezer would suffice, with the large unit in an adjacent pantry.

Storing small appliances in a base cabinet can be very useful, provided you have ample storage for pots and pans and other items that take priority. This is where a separate storage pantry can be very handy.

Palm Beach Lifestyle

MEDITERRANEAN REVIVAL | PALM BEACH, FLORIDA

White kitchens are classic, clean-looking, and easy to work with. Bold-colored kitchens, on the other hand, can be more of a challenge. But, if done well, they can have such visual drama and joy!

To use a strong color, you must be able to visualize how it will work in the space and pull it together with confidence. A vibrant color needs to be used proportionately to the size of the room, and balanced with other colors and textures so as not to overpower or underwhelm. You must also know your client well. Some may embrace color with a "go big or go home" attitude, while others may say "a little goes a long way."

This kitchen was for the Kips Bay Palm Beach Showhouse in Florida. Being a showhouse, I could be bold with the color choice. I knew a blue kitchen would be perfect for this Mediterranean Revival-style house, as it had the space, height, and light to handle the strong color. Designed as a family's second residence, the kitchen could be more relaxed than their primary home, and the blue makes for a bright and cheerful space to spend time in cooking or entertaining.

Knowing how much color to use and where requires an understanding of positive and negative space. I balanced Benjamin Moore's "Blue Dragon" on the cabinetry, rangehood, and entablature (the positive space), with light tones, soft texture, and dark timber throughout the rest of the kitchen (the negative space).

Cabinetry beneath the countertop comprises full-height doors and banks of drawers. Full-height doors are a better scale for a high-ceilinged room, as opposed to a combination of door and drawer. And a 1-inch rail, instead of 2-inch rail, between the banks of drawers is a more simplistic and delicate approach. The framing bead is inspired by Naumkeag, the estate of Joseph Choate in Stockbridge, Massachusetts, designed by Stanford White of McKim, Mead & White in 1885. It is elegant, timeless, and transitional, and I added long, slim handles to the cabinetry for a streamlined, modern edge.

The entablature integrates the kitchen into the architecture of the room, and the four-piece profile is also based on a crown molding by White. He had a great grasp of scale and detail in his millwork and moldings, while at the same time keeping it rather simple, which is the effect I wanted to be in harmony with this home.

The countertops and walls are executed in light tones and soft textures, serving as the negative space between the blue cabinetry and entablature. Dekton is a gorgeous and robust product used for the countertops, and the slab is cut into tiles for the backsplash to give a subtle detail. Linen wallpaper lends a soft tonal texture, and the simple pelmet is trimmed with brass studs.

If I can make a kitchen functional without overhead cabinets then I do, as it enhances the light and space in a room and provides more wall for displaying decorative artworks. A local Florida artist painted the images of the blue heron, which is indigenous to the area, and I added a pop of bright color to the corner with the orange trees. There is nothing better than orange and blue, and since it's Florida I had to have orange trees.

A solid block of tall blue cabinetry conceals the refrigerator on one wall. Tall cabinetry with blue frames and faux suede flanks the wine room on another wall, adding texture and another decorative element to break up the blue panels. The dark gray shelving in the wine room is warm and subdued and sets a sophisticated mood.

A wonderful antique French tailor's table serves as the kitchen island and adds depth and richness to balance the vibrancy of the room. I love to add in pieces with age and patina for character. Scale plays an important role in the height and size of a kitchen island as it can make a room feel smaller or larger. This table is narrow and lower than a typical island, so it doesn't dominate the space, and the lower height makes it more comfortable to work on. The handmade brass pendant light above is fun and bright and shimmers with the sunlight, and the clay olive jars beneath speak to the Mediterranean-style architecture of the house.

This kitchen is a fresh and cheerful room to spend time in. The contractor and workers questioned the blue cabinetry when it arrived, but the room just sang when it was completed, as I knew it would. It felt as though we had brought those blue skies right into the room! It exudes warmth and happiness and is perfect for a family's second residence or winter home.

PALM BEACH LIFESTYLE 163

Pro Tips

Be creative and cohesive with color, texture, and scale

Color and texture are fun kitchen design tools. However, ensuring they all work together is imperative. Use balance, proportion, and scale to bring them together.

Have fun with color, be creative, mix it up! Color can always be changed if you tire of it. However, the layout is harder to change, so get the groundwork right from the start.

The "everything in moderation" principle guides my designs. Color is a magnificent tool, especially when addressed through this framework. It is always a delicate balance of positive and negative space.

Textured materials can provide warmth and a tactile contrast to blocks of color.

Proportion and scale play an integral role, not only for color, but the size of furniture. An island does not need to be 36 inches high like the rest of the countertops. A lower island can provide an ideal ergonomic height for stirring, baking, and other tasks. It can also offer a greater sense of space and openness.

Mediterranean Moroccan

SPANISH REVIVAL | NEW ROCHELLE, NEW YORK

While there exist many reasons to undertake a project, I believe the most important is to know that the client you are working with is kind, understanding, and collaborative in transforming their home to fit their vision. This client embodied these qualities perfectly. She is absolutely lovely and a pleasure to work with.

The owners remained in their Spanish Revival home throughout the duration of the project. Living amid a major renovation can be extremely stressful, especially for a young family. Despite the chaotic environment, the owners handled this project with a sense of humor, maintaining a positive mindset and atmosphere regardless of the daunting construction process. They showed resilience as they moved into different parts of the home to allow for construction to move around. For the record, I do not recommend this to any of my clients. The client has my utmost respect, as she pressed on through this experience while raising three children and teaching.

Architect Herbert Feuerstein referred her to me, and she came with a distinct image of her hopes for the finalized project, which included 13-foot-high ceilings. My job was to accept the challenge of extrapolating the desired aesthetic in order to create her dream kitchen (and keep in mind her ceilings are 8 to 10 feet high).

A warm, soft white against the wood floor became the background and set the stage for the design. One of the client's many focal points was the kitchen island. She wanted it to be striking and made of wood. Tiger maple immediately came to mind to provide the pizazz she was seeking. Tiger maple is a beautiful warm wood, perfect as an accent piece.

Before the design process could begin, we had to start with an inspirational foundation. Inspiration comes from many different places, and the Institute of Classical Architecture & Art is often my go-to. However, the New York Armory hosts an annual art and antique show, which might be the only environment that beats the ICAA in this regard.

There, you will find the most beautiful antiques, from art and artifacts to furniture. The show offers the absolute best that money can buy, and perusing this exquisite collection provides the perfect access to enviable pieces of the highest quality. This is where I found the great inspiration for the design of the ends of the kitchen island.

I stumbled upon a piece of furniture comprising two different species of wood. The ends were walnut with an exotic veneer drawer base. The combination of the wood tones, along with the perfect proportions immediately caught my eye. I studied the piece carefully and walked away knowing exactly how I wanted to design the showstopping island.

Translating this inspiration into a functional design required a great deal of tweaking since the scale of the island is much larger than a piece of furniture. From the thickness and tapering of the legs to the overall height, the differences were vast. All these important details needed to be dealt with accordingly to create the dream island. The 1/8-inch raise from the main island created a frame providing "book ends" that give the island a greater importance.

I hesitated when my client requested a wood countertop in addition to the wood island. Educating clients on otherwise unknown aspects of kitchen design is an important obligation of my profession. I have the responsibility to make a kitchen beautiful, however, it must be functional at the same time. Knowing this family's active lifestyle and frequent cooking, I initially tried to talk her out of a wood countertop as it would likely be scratched up in a short period of time. But her desire to have this specific design became apparent, and I continued researching different finishes for a possible solution. My goal was to find a finish that would strengthen the countertop without looking like a plastic coat. After careful research, I came across a product that would withstand some punishment, and we decided to go for it.

Besides the striking wood kitchen island, my client's image for her kitchen was of a simple, modern appearance. This would provide a light backdrop to the room and focus attention on the island. We selected quartzite for the countertop, as it provided warmth and depth while still being extremely practical and durable. The backsplash provided the perfect opportunity to utilize a decorative mosaic tile, evocative of the home's original aesthetic. The custom-made ceramic mosaic tile was well worth the wait, and the color ties in beautifully with the wood island and custom hood beautifully.

Pro Tips

Design for your client's needs and taste

Kitchens serve a standard set of functions, but they should be designed specifically for a client's needs and taste, and every effort should be made to achieve their vision. A cook's kitchen functions very differently than a family kitchen.

A custom-designed island can make a kitchen truly unique. Inspiration can be found in many places. I personally find inspiration in historical houses, classical architecture, and antique shows. Antique furniture can be transformed into a kitchen island without a lot of effort, and provide a unique look.

Wooden countertops are not a first choice as they will scratch. Most mill shops are not well versed in a durable non-toxic countertop finish as it is a specialty item. Do your research to find suitable products and test them extensively to ensure they are up to the task and do what the supplier or manufacturer says. Also take care of them.

The backsplash is a perfect place to add decorative flair. It should still complement the kitchen design, and respect the home's original aesthetic.

MEDITERRANEAN MOROCCAN

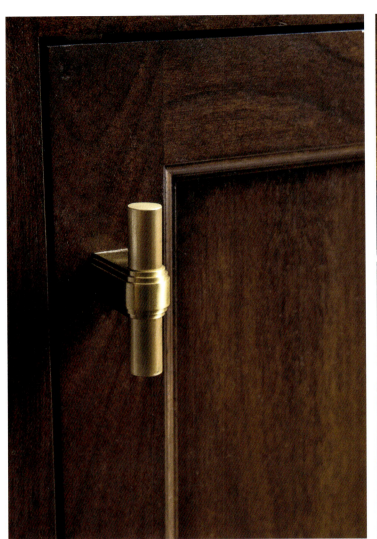

Storage was a key factor in this kitchen, as the family is kosher and adhered to strict storing guidelines. I love designing kosher kitchens as every element is doubled. Through meticulous planning, I ensured there would be enough storage space for two sets of everything: pots, pans, dishes, utensils, and so on. Being kosher, the client also required two large sinks. We installed these side by side beneath the window on the long countertop. Each sink has its own dishwasher, and the trash is between the two sinks.

Friday night dinners are a special time to spend with family and friends. The butler's pantry is important to support the use of the dining room during these events, and it should be beautiful to serve from and entertain. The custom faux walls are a stunning cobalt blue and provide a stark contrast to the kitchen. The warmth of the wood cabinets and luster of the open shelves create a warm and inviting atmosphere. The paneled backsplash with the brass center panels are unique additions that add character.

This kitchen and butler's pantry came together spectacularly. I enjoy visiting and seeing this family in action. A rewarding benefit after a job well done.

Gracious Georgian Home

GEORGIAN | STAMFORD, CONNECTICUT

I have always said that classicism is not a style. It's a language of rules that one abides by to produce a result that is harmonious, pleasing to the eye, and functional. The classical language in this 1900s Georgian home stands true.

Phillip James Dodd is a classical architect I admire greatly. I met him when he worked with Fairfax & Sammons. I know his foundation in the language is strong and that working with him is a pleasure. When Phillip asked me to design this kitchen I knew I could communicate and collaborate with him with ease.

There are two interesting aspects to this kitchen and wet bar: There is a more modern approach to the style, and it is a kosher kitchen. Thus, the two sinks have a major responsibility as there is a meat section and a dairy section. Both are equally important and located in such a way that the work triangle is comfortable and flows. Since this client serves mostly meat for dinner, the meat sink is in the work triangle, positioned in front of the range. As dairy is more likely served for breakfast and lunch, it is positioned across the countertop from the range, as it is not used as much.

My client does a lot of cooking, but did not wish to see a lot of stainless steel. The Sub-Zero tower units are clean and present themselves as a paneled wall; you would never know they are there. They are also extremely functional, as they have a Sabbath mode.

I always defer back to the greats of yesteryear for millwork as their simplistic profiles endure. They are classic and timeless and the kitchen will always stay in style. Complemented with wood floors, Danby marble countertops, and beautiful Nanz hardware, this kitchen is truly classic.

Many older homes do not have tall ceilings, so the proportions play a huge role in designing the kitchen. I must think through cabinet heights, and I don't want a rangehood to feel squat. It should have a sense of importance, and verticality will help.

A powder-coated stainless hood to match the cabinetry maintains a clean, understated, and continuous look and yet is a non-combustible, functional material. The polished nickel accents provide a simple aesthetic and a bit of brightness. The metal backsplash and the polished nickel bands complement one another and add some pizazz.

The butler's pantry is a little jewel. I used tiger maple wood, which is rich and catches the eye. The unusual tiger stripe look to the grain is achieved by how the lumber is cut, and it presents with great contrast when stained. I like to suggest this wood for special areas or an accent area. In this case the butler's pantry was the perfect location. To stay in the character of the home, we chose the sumptuous black and gold countertops as a dramatic complement to the stained wood. My design team selected custom French Cube lights to bring in a modern touch, and the reflective gloss of the ceiling brings such a glow.

I do believe that as wonderful and easy as premade wine units are, they do not have the character of custom ones. I wanted these wine units to be really special, and to have the feeling of a wine room rather than a wine appliance. By having the mill shop custom make them, they are far more integral to the overall character of the space and lend a wonderful, layered quality.

This project was a perfect collaboration from start to finish, and the harmony between Phillip and my own design team is reflected in the harmonious result.

Pro Tips
Design with restraint

Selection of hardware prior to fabricating millwork is critical. The size of rails on drawer fronts can have a direct impact on the size of hardware, so plan ahead.

A stone or glass backsplash offers a more modern look than tiles or wood panels.

Space planning is necessary when a sink and range are back-to-back. There needs to be efficient countertop and circulation area between the range, sink, and refrigerator.

The style of hinge will simplify or embellish one's kitchen aesthetic. A concealed hinge is a more modern approach, versus an exposed hinge, which is a more traditional approach.

GRACIOUS GEORGIAN HOME 189

Classically Detailed in Darien

CLASSICAL | DARIEN, CONNECTICUT

By now, reading about these kitchens, you will have surmised that I am constantly educating myself in the classical language of architecture, the importance of space planning, and the nuances of fine architectural millwork. Together, they lay the foundation for a functional, beautiful kitchen that works in the twenty-first century.

This home in Darien is one of my favorite projects. It not only required a great deal of spatial forethought, but also allowed me to integrate very precisely thought-out architectural millwork into the space.

The needs of the homeowner always come first, and it is imperative to know their requirements for the room prior to laying out the space. The next priority is understanding the details, and how they will contribute to meeting the goals for the room. This is how we define, determine, and support a guiding aesthetic. Details make or break the success of a design. Each component must relate to the other, to the space it is designed in, and to the overall aesthetic of the architecture.

The function of this kitchen needed to work for the client who is a wonderful cook. A chef is trained to work in a very tight triangle—that simple turn or pivot from sink to range or refrigerator is all they need to function best. So this efficient triangle came to the forefront in designing the layout for this kitchen. Everything is close to hand or within a few steps reach, and the Viking range with the open burner concept is a real workhorse.

Many nineteenth-century homes have a summer beam running through the center of the structure. The design of this kitchen started at the ceiling down, so the summer beam became part of the aesthetic, with the cabinetry seamlessly integrated into the room's interior architecture. The color and design of the white cabinetry showcases my client's blue china, which is complemented by a patterned blue-and-white backsplash.

Historic details bring more aesthetic charm. The German silver custom sink returns us to a yesteryear feeling, yet is large enough to handle any task. And the Belgium bluestone floor is easy to clean and very durable.

CLASSICALLY DETAILED IN DARIEN 193

Inspiration for the architectural millwork in the butler's pantry came from McKim, Mead & White's use of quarter-sawn and rift white oak and their impeccable attention to detail. The wall cabinet's sliding doors of light restoration glass feel true to the period, and provide a wonderful showcase for the display of more china and other heirlooms.

Off the kitchen, the breakfast room has a more formal atmosphere. A reclaimed French parquet oak floor with a French wax finish complements the nineteenth-century-inspired custom millwork I designed for the fine dishes and storage. Tiger maple-stained cabinets with a black-and-gold marble countertop and backsplash are timeless and imbue a little glamour into the room.

CLASSICALLY DETAILED IN DARIEN 199

The library, with its aged walnut and crotch walnut door, demanded a French polish finish. The eighteenth-century details of fine architectural millwork resonate in this space. Old-style ratchet shelf supports are beautiful to me, and easy to adjust. I saw this detail in a very old library and wondered why it is not used more today. I find that fighting with the typical brass pegs used for adjustable shelving today is more difficult than to maneuver on my own.

I love the look of the old plaster on the walls and suggested that we not paint them. We waxed the plaster after it cured, which allows for easy care and an aged, warm look. The plank French oak waxed floors complement the parquet floor of the breakfast room.

This house provided a wonderful opportunity to meld my love and appreciation of classical elements with the functionality needed for a modern kitchen.

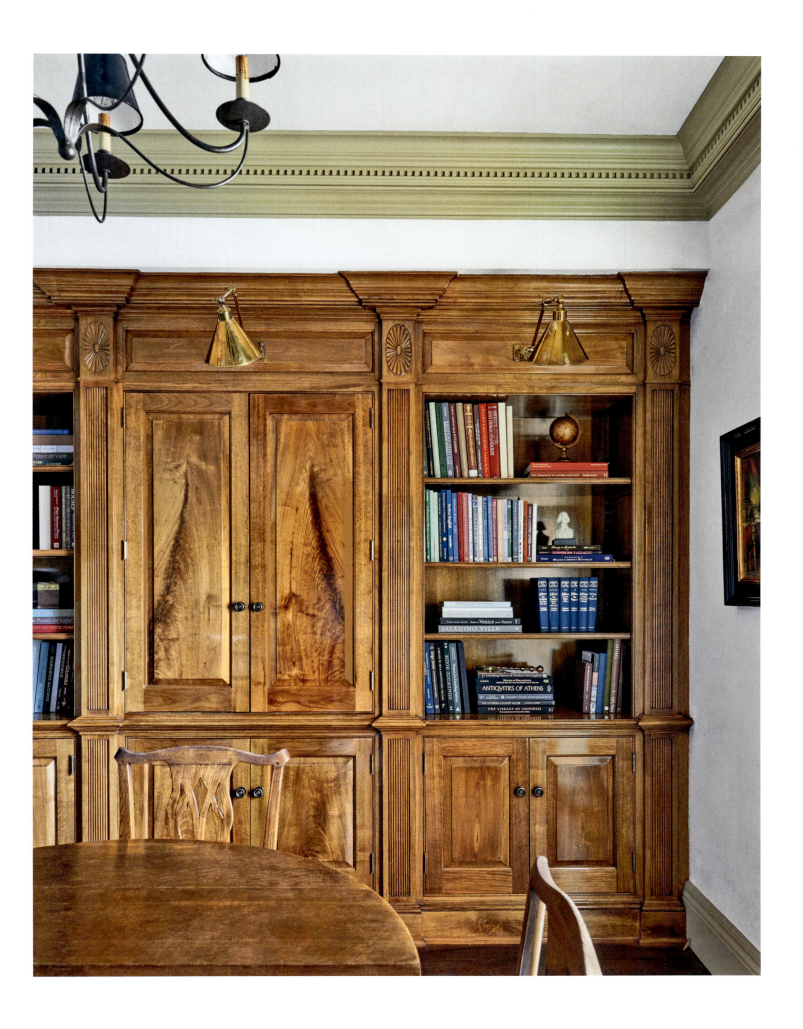

CLASSICALLY DETAILED IN DARIEN

Pro Tips
Integrate millwork into the architecture

Millwork needs to be designed specifically to integrate within the architecture of a kitchen or any room in a home.

Finetuning the proportions in millwork is always a delicate balance, particularly the overall height of an entablature, the proportions of the wall cabinets to the height of the counter, and the height of the backsplash. All parts make up the whole, and each room can vary greatly.

Stained architectural millwork starts with the selection of the wood. The quality, the width of the boards, and how the boards are joined will be important factors in the beauty for a successful outcome.

Woods change as they age and acquire a patina. American walnut is one of the few woods that gets lighter with age. The older it gets, the more seasoned and beautiful it is.

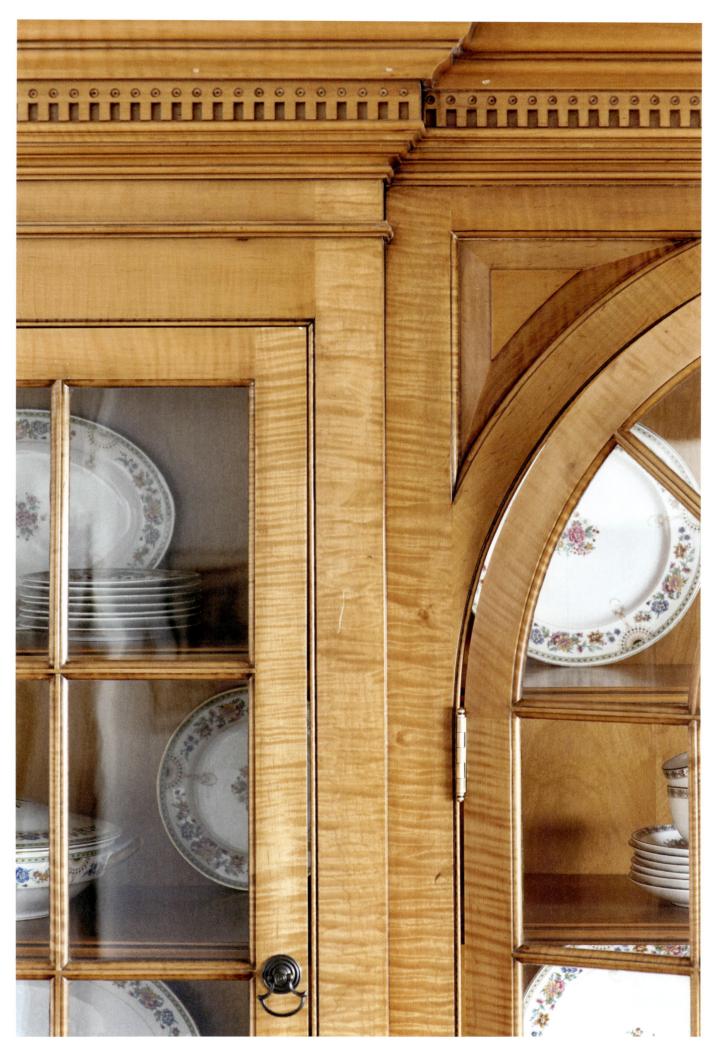

CLASSICALLY DETAILED IN DARIEN

American Farmhouse Dream

AMERICANA | NEW CANAAN, CONNECTICUT

Nestled on a small hill in New Canaan, Connecticut, lies our former family home, where Charles and I raised our son David. It's where I started my design studio, and where I embraced my love of Americana architecture. I was able to exercise this passion through transforming the small 1957 Cape-style house into a warm, beautiful, and modest home with the simplicity and naïveté of a New England farmhouse, and to accommodate a growing family.

My passion for historic architecture has guided me through most of my design career, and classical architecture and the American farmhouse hold a special place in my heart. I am always drawn to architectural roots as a starting point to drive the aesthetic of a project. Inspired by *Architectural Treasures of Early America* and *Big House, Little House, Back House, Barn*, I designed an 1,800-square-foot addition with the windows, moldings, and millwork of an eighteenth-century farmhouse. These architectural trims and characteristics provide vital clues to the age of a house. With 12-over-12 windows and small panes of glass reminiscent of yesteryear, as well as classical pilasters embellishing the front door, our house appeared as though it had stood there since New England's early days.

In keeping with this theme of celebrating the past, I used natural materials that would develop a patina, becoming even more beautiful with age. Reclaimed gumwood flooring from an old Southern tobacco barn has been tung oiled. Hand-hewn ceiling beams give logic to the kitchen and family room, and wheat and mica mixed into the plaster implement a pretty texture and subtle reflective finish on the walls. In the 1700s, horsehair was used as a bridging agent to control the shrinking of the plaster.

The butternut wood on the cabinets is native to Eastern North America and one of the most beautiful timbers. The grain and knots in the reclaimed butternut wood express character and age. Orion Henderson at Horton Brasses in Connecticut hand-forged the latch-and-bolt handles and rat-tail hinges characteristic of a New England farmhouse. Two large doors with long strap hinges conceal the refrigerator and a bulletin board where I kept my notes, invitations, and calendar, all within handy reach, but out of sight.

Charles and I love to cook, so we created a personal testing ground for a truly functional kitchen. The goal was to construct a space that would accommodate a professional chef or multiple cooks, allowing them to effectively and efficiently work together in the same space. Happy cooks and happy couples!

We each had our own workstations with sinks and shared the central table and cooktop. Charles did his food prep at the island sink that I had made as a gift for him. The structure became the focal point of the room and soon took on a life of its own. Inspired by old soapstone sinks, it had a deep sink, shallow sink, and ledge that we lined ingredients upon when we cooked. We filled the sinks with ice to chill beer, clams, shrimp, and appetizers when entertaining, and our family and friends gathered around the stone countertop, which we also used as a buffet.

I did my food prep at the double sink beneath the front window, admiring our English garden and eighteenth-century Delft tiles that I collected for the backsplash. The painted canvas rug in front of the sink was very fashionable in the olden days, but unfortunately, you don't see many of them today because they don't hold up well.

Charles and I shared the cooking island—a 32-inch-high antique table—and the cooktop beneath the acid-wash metal rangehood, which had a beautiful, rustic patina. The uncommon table-island provided a comfortable surface space to work on, especially since it stood on a lower plane than the rest of the prep stations.

AMERICAN FARMHOUSE DREAM

Our pantry had numerous functions, the most important being a small area for our two dogs to sleep. The blue-wash cabinetry with walnut countertops was a perfect complement to the antique gumwood walls. And the shelving brackets, settle bench, and tin lampshades are all reminiscent of an early New England home.

The kitchen faced the family room, which doubled in size over the course of the renovation. A niche materialized where the structural beam was to be installed, producing the perfect fit for my antique Welsh cupboard from the Stair Galleries auction house in Hudson, New York. The old leather chairs, also purchased at auction, completed the matured look, with the carpet providing a neutral backdrop. Shiplap was used in many old homes long before HGTV existed. The vertically hung shiplap is painted "China White," by Benjamin Moore, a clean palette for any style.

I felt maintaining the 12-over-12 windows was important throughout the home. This included multi-lite windows installed along the entire back wall to bring great eastern light in to flood the space. We spent our summers in this room and on the terrace soaking in the sun. Conversely, our winters were spent in front of the fireplace in the living room.

The living room opens to the neighboring dining room, delineated with a geometric ceiling pattern inspired by a McKim, Mead & White home. I explicitly did not create large coffers, as I find them to be overused and many times too large for a room. In a house with lower ceilings, adding a pattern that only drops down an inch added formality and charm, and defined the space separate from the living room, without reducing height or inserting a wall for delineation.

The front foyer was proportionate to the home. However, the long, expansive living room was larger than necessary. Since there were no front hall closets, I designed a paneled jamb with a wide opening into the living room. The structure added 12 feet of closet space; 6 feet on each side. This created a grander entry to the living room as well as newfound, functional storage space.

I designed this home with the sentiment that it would be our forever home. When Charles and I eventually sold the house in 2016, we were thrilled to hear Debbie Propst, president of One Kings Lane at the time and now with Herman Miller, had bought it. I knew she would love spending time with her family and friends in this phenomenal home, as our family had for so many years prior. I believe good memories make for good karma!

Pro Tips
Design your own dream kitchen

Designing your own kitchen is an opportunity to embrace your true passion. My dream kitchen was a celebration of the past, and it holds a special place in my heart.

Natural materials that develop a patina become even more beautiful with age and wear. The hood in this kitchen is an acid-washed metal, which is a live finish, so it will continue to change in color as time goes on. Waxing the metal hood will minimize the oxidation process. The reclaimed wood for the cabinetry and flooring already has graining and knots that express their character and age. Leathered Verdi Quasai granite for the countertops and sink has beautiful color and veining and is strong enough to withstand the abuse from day-to-day use.

Custom details will reflect your taste and passion. I had the drawer pulls, latch-and-bolt handles, and rat-tail hinges hand-forged by Orion Henderson at Horton Brasses in Connecticut. My father loved to make furniture, and I remember visiting the Horton Brasses factory as a young child with him. The backsplash is made of eighteenth-century sepia Delft tiles I collected one by one.

Acknowledgments

I so often say that it takes a village, and to write this book I have had the most incredible village that I wish to thank:

First, my mother and father, Mary and Sam, who exposed me to culture and travels throughout my childhood, and believed that education is the top priority in one's life.

Of course, my husband and son, Charles and David, who are always supporting me. They both mean so much to me.

To Anne Fairfax and Richard Sammons, who welcomed me into the Institute of Classical Architecture & Art in 1994. I have learned so much through the ICAA and have never been so passionate about an organization. The classical language has, and will always be, a part of my life and my design work.

To Bunny Williams, who I have had the honor to work with for more than twenty years. Bunny has been a great mentor, teacher, collaborator, and friend.

To Ellen Niven of NivenBreen, who helped make this book possible with my busy schedule. Ellen allowed me to continue my daily work and guided me through the process of preparing the manuscript.

To Nicole Boehringer and The Images Publishing Group. Nicole's talent and unbelievable patience guided me through the process as well.

And most of all, I must thank my clients who gave me the opportunity to work on these wonderful projects. I love what I do and enjoy each and every project, bringing my clients' kitchens to life.

Thank you all.

Sarah

Project Credits

Picturesque Family Heirlooms

Location: Litchfield Hills, Connecticut
Photography: Neil Landino Photography
Architecture: Ferguson & Shamamian Architects
Interior design: Bunny Williams Interior Design
Kitchen and pantry design: Sarah Blank Design Studio, LLC
Millwork design: Sarah Blank Design Studio, LLC
Contractor: Jacob Bump

MATERIALS, APPLIANCES, AND FITTINGS

Millwork paint: Farrow & Ball "Cornforth White"
Countertops: Gascogne Grey limestone
Backsplash: Mosaic House, Moroccan tiles; bead board
Clean-up sink and prep sink: Julien Sinks
Clean-up sink faucet: Franke
Prep-sink faucet: Franke
Clean-up sink dishwasher: Miele, fully integrated
Prep-sink dishwasher: Fisher & Paykel
Refrigerator: Sub-Zero, fully integrated
Freezer: Sub-Zero, drawers
Range: Caliber Appliances, all-gas, 48", Indoor Professional
High-speed oven: Miele
Single oven: Miele, combi steam
Warming drawer: Miele, fully integrated
Hood: Custom stainless-steel acid washed with custom strapping and brass
Decorative hardware: Classic Brass
Pendant lights: BWI
Copper: Client's personal collection
Artwork: Client's personal collection

Majestic Hudson River Valley

Location: Irvington, New York
Photography: Neil Landino Photography
Design: Sarah Blank Design Studio, LLC
Millwork: Sarah Blank Design Studio, LLC
Contractor: Taconic Builders

MATERIALS, APPLIANCES, AND FITTINGS

KITCHEN

Millwork paint: Farrow & Ball "Dimity" and "Stone Blue"
Countertops: ABC Worldwide Stone, Lapitec sintered stone
Main sink: Texas Lightsmith
Main faucet: Waterworks
Pot filler: Waterworks
Dishwasher: Miele, fully integrated
Refrigerator: Sub-Zero, 36" tower, fully integrated
Freezer: Sub-Zero, 30" tower, fully integrated
Range: Blue Star, all-gas range, 36"
High-speed oven: Miele
Hood: Sarah Blank Design Studio, LLC, custom copper and brass
Pendant lights, surface lights, and sconces: Paul Ferrante
Decorative hardware: Frank Allart
Furniture design and selection: Sarah Blank Design Studio, LLC
Table: IstDibs
Chairs: Palecek
Cushions: Schumacher
Pillows: Morris & Co.

PANTRY

Millwork: Quarter-sawn and rift white oak, custom stain
Countertop: ABC Worldwide Stone, Lapitec sintered stone
Sink: Texas Lightsmith
Refrigerator: Sub-Zero, fully integrated under counter
Wallpaper: Morris & Co.

Bridging the Past and Future

Location: Bronxville, New York
Photography: Neil Landino Photography
Architecture: Douglas C. Wright Architects
Interior design: Brian J McCarthy, Inc
Kitchen and butler's pantry design: Sarah Blank Design Studio, LLC
Millwork: Sarah Blank Design Studio, LLC
Contractor: Taconic Builders

MATERIALS, APPLIANCES, AND FITTINGS

Millwork: Quarter-sawn and rift white oak
Cabinet finish: Custom cerused oak
Countertops: Calacatta Gold marble
Backsplash: Urban Archaeology, Metal Urban Brass
Backsplash behind range: Custom brushed brass and brushed stainless steel
Sinks: Julien Sinks
Main faucet: Kallista
Island faucet: Julien Sinks
Dishwasher: Miele, fully integrated
Refrigerator: Miele, fully integrated
Freezer: Miele, fully integrated
Range top: Wolf Range, 48" wide
Steam oven: Miele
High-speed oven: Miele
Single wall oven: Miele
Hood: Sarah Blank Design Studio, LLC, custom brushed brass and brushed stainless steel
Hardware: Katonah Architectural Hardware
Floors: Existing white oak
Decorative hardware: Katonah Architectural Hardware

A Special Place in Bedford

Location: Bedford, New York
Photography: Stacy Bass Photography
Architecture: Fairfax & Sammons
Interior design: Sam Blount Inc.
Kitchen and pantry design: Sarah Blank Design Studio, LLC
Millwork design: Sarah Blank Design Studio, LLC
Contractor: A & S Contracting

MATERIALS, APPLIANCES, AND FITTINGS
KITCHEN
Millwork paint: Benjamin Moore, "Simply White"
Countertops: Soapstone
Main sink: Shaw Original
Main faucet: Perrin & Rowe
Dishwasher: Miele, fully integrated
Dishwasher: Miele Pro
Refrigerator: Viking
Refrigerated drawers: Sub-Zero
Freezer: Viking (in larder)
Freezer drawers: Sub-Zero
Range: Viking, all gas, 36" wide
Range: Viking, griddle, 24" wide
High-speed oven: Miele
Single oven: Miele
Decorative hardware: Bouvet
Light fixture: Sam Blount Inc.

BUTLER'S PANTRY
Millwork: White oak, custom stain
Countertops: Leathered black absolute
Sink and faucet: Rocky Mountain Hardware
Wine cooler: Sub-Zero

Mediterranean in Connecticut

Location: Darien, Connecticut
Photography: Stacy Bass Photography
Architecture: Sheldon Richard Kostelecky Architect
Design: Sarah Blank Design Studio, LLC
Millwork design: Sarah Blank Design Studio, LLC
Contractor: David Brown

MATERIALS, APPLIANCES, AND FITTINGS
Millwork: White oak, custom stain
Countertops: Perimeter Wood
Island: Carrara marble

Sink: Restored Monel sink
Faucets: Watermark
Range: AGA Range
Antique dish hutch: Lillian August
Beams: Antique (reclaimed)
Floor: Tumbled limestone
Decorative hardware: Bouvet
Chandelier over island: Client
Table and chairs: Antiques

A Classic Beauty

Location: Scarsdale, New York
Photography: Stacy Bass Photography
Kitchen, pantry, and master bath design: Sarah Blank Design Studio, LLC
Millwork design: Sarah Blank Design Studio, LLC

MATERIALS, APPLIANCES, AND FITTINGS
KITCHEN
Millwork paint: Benjamin Moore, "Dove White"
Countertops: Taj Mahal quartzite
Glass backsplash: Custom Bendheim glass
Sinks: Julien Sinks
Faucets: Perrin & Rowe
Dishwasher: Miele Pro
Dishwasher: Miele, fully integrated
Refrigerator: Sub-Zero 48" Pro
Freezer: Sub-Zero Pro
Range: Wolf Range, 60" wide
Steam oven: Miele
High-speed oven: Miele
Hood: Custom stainless with stainless straps
Hardware: Hamilton Sinkler
Hinges: Brusso Hardware
Pendant lights: Vaughan
Surface-mounted lights: Urban Archaeology
Stools: Client
Pacific drawer for silver: Custom

BUTLER'S PANTRY
Custom millwork: Tiger maple, custom stain
Countertops: Taj Mahal quartzite
Backsplash: Bendheim
Sink: Rocky Mountain
Faucet: Rocky Mountain
Wine Refrigerator: Sub-Zero
Refrigerator: Sub-Zero drawers
Hardware: Hamilton Sinkler

MASTER BATH:
Paint: Farrow & Ball, "Blackened"
Countertops and shower walls: Statuary marble
Shower floor and water closet floor: Bardiglio marble
Etched glass walls: Custom
Floor: Artisan Tile, mosaic marble
Tub: Waterworks
Tub Faucet: Lefroy Brooks
Toilet: Toto with Toto Washlet
Shower door handle: Hamilton Sinkler
Hinges: Nanz
Sconces: Waterworks

Family Memories and Traditions

Location: Sharon, Connecticut
Photography: Stacy Bass Photography
Interior design: Sarah Blank Design Studio, LLC and client
Architectural interiors and addition: Sarah Blank Design Studio, LLC
Millwork design: Sarah Blank Design Studio, LLC
Contractor: Mies Sudaval

MATERIALS, APPLIANCES, AND FITTINGS
Millwork paint: Farrow & Ball, "Mouse's Back"
Walls: Plaster with wax skim coat
Countertops: Leathered black absolute
Island sink: Native Trails
Island faucet: KWC
Dishwasher: Miele, fully integrated
Refrigerator: Sub-Zero, 30" Tower
Freezer: Sub-Zero, 30" Tower
Wine unit: Sub-Zero, under counter
Range: Wolf, all-gas range with open burners, 36" wide
High-speed oven: Miele
Single oven: Miele
Hood: Sarah Blank Design Studio, LLC, custom powder-coated standing seam black hood
Decorative hardware: Harwington
Style of cabinet: Lip door
Pendant lights: Authentic Designs
Dining room floor paint: Old Village Paint, "Kittenhouse Red"

WINE CELLAR
Wine storage: Custom, using existing wood from framing of the house
Floors: Slate
Walls: Antique barn boards

MASTER CLOSET AND BATH
Paint: Farrow & Ball, "Cornforth"
Plumbing: Jado Plumbing Fixtures
Countertops: Gascogne Grey limestone
Medicine cabinets: Robern
Furniture: Antiques

Transformed and Treasured

Location: Darien, Connecticut
Photography: Neil Landino Photography
Interior design: Sarah Blank Design Studio, LLC
Millwork design: Sarah Blank Design Studio, LLC

MATERIALS, APPLIANCES, AND FITTINGS
Custom millwork: Sarah Blank Design Studio, LLC
Countertops: Luna White quartzite
Backsplash: Luna White quartzite
Sinks: Julien Sinks
Faucets: Franke
Dishwasher: Miele, fully integrated
Refrigerator: Sub-Zero Column
Freezer: Sub-Zero Column
Range: Thermador, 36" wide
High-speed oven: Miele Combi
High-speed steam oven: Miele Combi
Hood: Sarah Blank Design Studio, LLC, custom stainless-steel hood with stainless-steel strapping
Decorative hardware: Top Knobs
Pendant lights: Remains Lighting
Chandelier over table: Remains Lighting
Table and chairs: Client's heirlooms

French Revival with Flair

Location: Darien, Connecticut
Photography: Neil Landino Photography
Architecture: Elizabeth Rogami at DV Architect
Interior design: Susan Thorn Interiors
Kitchen and pantry design: Sarah Blank Design Studio, LLC and client

MATERIALS, APPLIANCES, AND FITTINGS
Countertops: Imperial Danby marble
Island countertop: Zinc
Backsplash: Solar Antique Tiles

Sink: Julien Sinks
Faucets: Perrin & Rowe
Dishwasher: Miele, fully integrated
Refrigerator: Miele, fully integrated
Freezer: Miele
Range: Blue Star Rangetop, 48" wide
Double wall oven: Miele, fully integrated
High-speed oven: Miele Combi
Steam oven: Miele Combi
Hood: Sarah Blank Design Studio, LLC, custom zinc
Decorative hardware: Rocky Mountain Hardware
Fireback: Client

Palm Beach Lifestyle

Location: Palm Beach, Florida
Photography: Brantley Photography
Kitchen and pantry design: Sarah Blank Design Studio, LLC
Millwork design: Sarah Blank Design Studio, LLC

MATERIALS, APPLIANCES, AND FITTINGS
Millwork: Recessed panel with custom framing bead
Millwork paint: Benjamin Moore, "Blue Dragon"
Ceiling paint: Benjamin Moore, "Blue Dragon," cut 50%
Wine room paint: Benjamin Moore, "Dragon's Breath"
Countertops: Dekton by Cosentino
Sink: Kohler
Faucet: Kallista
Appliances: Thermador
Decorative hardware: Palm Beach Classic Hardware
Light fixture in kitchen: Remains Lighting
Light fixture in wine room: Currey & Company
Leather: Fabricut
Antique tailor table: Authentic Provence
Kitchen runner: Sacco Carpet
Wall covering: Carlisle & Company
Artwork: Axiom Fine Art
Window treatment: The Shade Store
Wine room rug: New Moon Rug
Accessories: Devonshire of Palm Beach, Mecox Garden

Mediterranean Moroccan

Location: New Rochelle, New York
Photography: Leslie Unruh
Kitchen design: Sarah Blank Design Studio, LLC
Millwork design: Sarah Blank Design Studio, LLC

MATERIALS, APPLIANCES, AND FITTINGS
Millwork paint: Benjamin Moore, "Chantilly Lace"
Countertops: Taj Mahal quartzite, honed
Island countertop: Grothouse, walnut with Durata finish
Island wood: Tiger maple with custom stain
Island legs: Walnut with custom stain
Backsplash: Mosaic House
Sinks: Julien Sinks
Faucets: Kohler
Refrigerator: Sub-Zero, fully integrated
Double wall oven: Wolf
Hood: Sarah Blank Design Studio, LLC, custom walnut with brass trim
Decorative hardware: Amec Martin
Pendant light fixture: 1stDibs
Pendant light over table: Urban Electric
Window treatments: The Shade Store
Stools: Client
Table and chairs: LM Design

BUTLER'S PANTRY
Millwork: Walnut
Countertops: Grothouse, tiger maple
Sink: Texas Lightsmith
Wine cooler: Sub-Zero
Wall finishes: Heidi Holzer
Open shelves: Amuneal
Decorative hardware: Amec Martin

Gracious Georgian Home

Location: Stamford, Connecticut
Photography: Leslie Unruh
Architecture: Phillip James Dodd Architect
Interior design: Sarah Blank Design Studio, LLC
Millwork design: Sarah Blank Design Studio, LLC
Contractor: Cum Laude Group

MATERIALS, APPLIANCES, AND FITTINGS
KITCHEN
Perimeter paint: Donald Kaufman, "DKC-51"
Island paint: Farrow & Ball, "Light Grey"
Countertop and backsplash: Imperial Danby marble, honed

Backsplash behind hood: Urban Archaeology, metal tiles
Sinks: Julien Sinks
Faucets: Kallista
Dishwasher: Miele, fully integrated
Refrigerator and freezer: Sub-Zero, fully integrated
Refrigerator: True, fully integrated under-counter
Range: Blue Star, open burner range, 36" wide
High-speed oven: Miele
Steam oven: Miele Combi
Hood: Sarah Blank Design Studio, LLC, custom polished nickel 1/8-by-1/8" detail with a powder coat metal
Decorative hardware: Nanz
Pendant light: Studio Van Den Akker
Hinges: Brusso Hardware
Island stools: Modernlink
Shades: Zak + Fox

BUTLER'S PANTRY
Millwork: Tiger maple, custom stained
Ceiling paint: Benjamin Moore, "Midnight Dream," high gloss
Countertops: Black/gold marble
Sink and faucet: Rocky Mountain
Custom wine units: Sarah Blank Design Studio, LLC
Icemaker: True ice machine, concealed
Decorative hardware: Nanz
Surface-mounted lights: Atelier Jean Perzel
Pendant light: Apparatus Studio
Paneled jamb: Harmon Hinge, concealed
Hinges: Nanz

BREAKFAST ROOM
Table and chairs: Fair Design
Wallpaper: Phillip Jeffries
Light fixture: Allied Lighting
Window treatments: Zak + Fox

Classically Detailed in Darien

Location: Darien, Connecticut
Photography: Curtis Ryan Lew Photography
Design: Sarah Blank Design Studio, LLC and Sam Blount Inc.
Interior architecture and custom millwork: Sarah Blank Design Studio, LLC
Contractor: Sarah Blank Design Studio, LLC

MATERIALS, APPLIANCES, AND FITTINGS
KITCHEN
Millwork paint: Benjamin Moore, "China White"
Countertops: Gascogne Grey limestone
Backsplash: Custom butterfly board
Sink: German Silver Sink Company
Faucet: Perrin & Rowe
Dishwasher: Miele, fully integrated
Refrigerator and freezer: Sub-Zero
Range: Viking
Pendant light over island: Berkshire Antiques
Floor: Belgian Bluestone

BUTLER'S PANTRY
Millwork: Quarter-sawn and rift white oak, custom stain
Sink: Antique Monel sink restored
Faucet: Perrin & Rowe
Countertops: Carrara marble and rift oak
Floor: Carrara marble, honed
Table: Antique
Dishes and accessories: Antiques

BREAKFAST ROOM
Millwork: Tiger maple, custom stain
Countertop and backsplash: Black-and-gold marble
Floor: Reclaimed French parquet oak, French wax finish

LIBRARY
Custom millwork: Walnut, crotch walnut for center doors
Finish: Custom French polish finish
Floors: Reclaimed French oak, waxed
Walls: Plaster, cured and waxed
Desk, table, and chair: Antiques

American Farmhouse Dream

Location: New Canaan, Connecticut
Photography: Curtis Ryan Lew Photography
Design: Sarah Blank Design Studio, LLC and Sam Blount Inc.
Millwork design: Sarah Blank Design Studio, LLC
Contractor: Sarah Blank Design Studio, LLC

MATERIALS, APPLIANCES, AND FITTINGS
KITCHEN
Wood: Reclaimed butternut wood, Sutherland Welles stain
Countertop: Leathered Verdi Quasai granite
Backsplash: Eighteenth-century sepia Delft tiles
Sink: Stone custom-built leathered Verdi Quasai
Sinks under the windows: Julien Sinks
Faucets: Moen
Faucet at stone sink: KWC
Dishwashers: Miele
Range: Viking, all gas
Single wall oven: Thermador
High-speed oven: Miele, concealed
Hood: Custom acid-washed standing seam metal with acid-washed backsplash and shelf
Decorative hardware: Horton Brasses
Copper surface mounted lights: Auction
Floor: Carlisle Wide Plank Floors, reclaimed gumwood
Walls: Custom plaster with wheat mixed in for texture
Cooking island: Antique table
Antique American flag: Jeff Bridgeman
Antiques: Personal collection
Hand painted canvas rigs: Canvasworks, by artist Lisa Curry Mair

BUTLER'S PANTRY
Countertop: Walnut with tongue oil finish
Walls: Carlisle Wide Plank Floors, antique gumwood
Steam oven: Miele, concealed
Settle: Antique
Copper lights: PW Vintage Lighting
Flooring: Slate
Antiques: Personal collection

FAMILY ROOM
Rug: Custom sisal
Leather chairs: James Julia Auction
English Welsh cupboard: Stair Galleries
Sofas and dining room chairs: Sam Blount Inc.
Towle lamp: James D. Julia Auction
Dining room chairs: Regency, Sam Blount Inc.
Dining room table: Custom-made by a furniture maker in Lancaster, PA
English corner hutch: Guilford Antiques

LIVING ROOM
Sofa: James D. Julia Auction, covered with antique linen
Club chairs: Sam Blount Inc.
Mirror over fireplace: Pook & Pook, Inc., Shelley collection
Leather chair: Heirloom, custom-covered in Edelman Leather with keystone pattern

Published in Australia in 2022 by
The Images Publishing Group Pty Ltd
ABN 89 059 734 431

Offices

Melbourne
6 Bastow Place
Mulgrave, Victoria 3170
Australia
Tel: +61 3 9561 5544

New York
6 West 18th Street 4B
New York, NY 10011
United States
Tel: +1 212 645 1111

Shanghai
6F, Building C, 838 Guangji Road
Hongkou District, Shanghai 200434
China
Tel: +86 021 31260822

books@imagespublishing.com
www.imagespublishing.com

Copyright © The Images Publishing Group Pty Ltd 2022
The Images Publishing Group Reference Number: 1552

All photography is attributed in the Project Credits on pages 221–24, unless otherwise noted.
Page 2: Brantley Photography (Palm Beach Lifestyle); page 6: Neil Landino Photography (Bridging the Past and Future); page 8: Neil Landino Photography (Picturesque Family Heirlooms); page 10: Stacy Bass Photography (A Special Place in Bedford); page 12: Neil Landino Photography (Majestic Hudson River Valley); page 14: Curtis Ryan Lew Photography (Classically Detailed in Darien); page 15: Leslie Unruh (Mediterranean Moroccan); page 16: Stacy Bass Photography (Mediterranean in Connecticut); pages 18–19: Fritz von der Schulenburg (Hollyhock, designed with Bunny Williams); pages 21 and 22: Melanie Acevedo (Hickory Hill, designed with Bunny Williams); End papers and Pro Tips backgrounds: Wallpaper design by Tom Maciag of Dyad Communications

All rights reserved. Apart from any fair dealing for the purposes of private study, research, criticism or review as permitted under the Copyright Act, no part of this publication may be reproduced, stored in a retrieval system or transmitted in any form by any means, electronic, mechanical, photocopying, recording or otherwise, without the written permission of the publisher.

A catalogue record for this book is available from the National Library of Australia

Title: Classic Kitchens for Modern Living: Sarah Blank Design Studio
ISBN: 9781864708677

This title was commissioned in IMAGES' Melbourne office and produced as follows: *Editorial* Georgia (Gina) Tsarouhas, Jeanette Wall, Rebecca Gross *Graphic design and production* Nicole Boehringer

Printed by Graphius nv, Belgium, on 150gsm Magno Matt art paper

IMAGES has included on its website a page for special notices in relation to this and its other publications.
Please visit www.imagespublishing.com
Every effort has been made to trace the original source of copyright material contained in this book.
The publishers would be pleased to hear from copyright holders to rectify any errors or omissions.
The information and illustrations in this publication have been prepared and supplied by Sarah Blank Design Studio.
While all reasonable efforts have been made to ensure accuracy, the publishers do not, under any circumstances, accept responsibility for errors, omissions and representations express or implied.